THE ART OF GRILLING

BY
KELLY McCUNE

DESIGN BY
THOMAS INGALLS

PHOTOGRAPHY BY
VIKTOR BUDNIK

FOOD STYLING BY
KAREN HAZARIAN

PERENNIAL LIBRARY

HARPER & ROW, PUBLISHERS, NEW YORK
Cambridge, Philadelphia, San Francisco, Washington
London, Mexico City, São Paulo, Singapore, Sydney

*Dedicated to the future grillers
of the world.*

ACKNOWLEDGEMENTS

Thanks to Biordi, Sue Fisher King, Cotton-wood, The Gardener, Williams Sonoma, Pottery Barn, Forrest Jones, The Ginsburg Collection, V. Breier, Cookin', Annie Glass, Jeff & Debi McMains of Hasty–Bake, and Richard Tully of AGFA Corp. Their assistance and support help make this book look the way it does.

To Alan Steed of Lazzari Fuel Company, Inc. for all the great mesquite charcoal.

To Jay Hanson at BSW, Inc. for the Imperial Kamado.

To Chuck Woodside of ABW, Inc. for use of various Weber grills.

To Sandra Cook, Eve Shaw, and Diane Elander for help with props.

To Suzanne Gottschang for her help with recipe testing and her excellent palate.

To Carolyn Miller for her ever-vigilant editing and proofing.

To Janie Celeste Hewson for her support.

Harper & Row, Publishers, Inc.
10 East 53rd Street
New York, NY 10022
Published simultaneously in Canada by Fitzhenry & Whiteside Limited, Toronto

Printed in Japan

Quotation on page 5 from *Barnes & Noble Book of Quotations (Revised and Enlarged)*. Copyright © 1987 by Fitzhenry & Whiteside Limited, Toronto. Reprinted by permission.

Book and Cover Design:
Thomas Ingalls + Associates
Photography and Set Design:
Viktor Budnik
Food Styling and Props:
Karen Hazarian
Prop Stylist:
Liz Ross
Assistant to the Photographer:
Carol Haagens
Assistant to the Stylist:
Gina Frances Farruggio

Library of Congress Cataloging-in-Publication Data available

91 92 10 9 8 7 6 5 4 3

I feel a recipe is only a theme,
which an intelligent cook can play
each time with a variation.
MADAME BENOIT

TABLE OF CONTENTS

INTRODUCTION

Since we published *Grill Book* almost four years ago, home grilling has drawn an ever-larger following, made up of those who are attracted to a healthful new cooking method as well as old barbecue hands with an interest in new techniques. As we knew then, grilling is not just a trend destined to fade. In fact, it has firmly rooted itself country-wide as an easy yet sophisticated cuisine.

Barbecuing, our true outdoor-cooking tradition, has never gone out of style in this country, not since it was first created for large-scale feasts and then popularized for the backyard barbecue in the late forties. Real barbecue requires long, slow cooking with wood smoke and tangy basting sauces. Grilling, or quick-cooking over hot coals, goes back at least as far as the backyard barbecue, but we've begun to grill other foods besides steaks and burgers, and vegetables have come out of their foil packets and onto the grill. We have rediscovered our rich culinary heritage in many regions of the United States: unique seasonings from the deep South, Kansas City barbecue, and the earthy cuisine of the Southwest. These are only some of the flavors that have influenced the sauces and marinades in *The Art of Grilling*. Relishes and condiments from different parts of the world have further expanded our grilling repertoire. It has been easy to incorporate these new ideas into our own barbecue heritage. Food from the grill will never cease to appeal, chiefly because it is hearty, delicious, *and* healthy.

The Art of Grilling complements *Grill Book* by offering more tips, more information on successful grilling, and an entirely new collection of recipes. Since new products have been created for the burgeoning grill market, the range of choices is greater for the home cook, and equipment can be tailored to individual needs. You can read up on the options available before investing money. More high-quality charcoals are available now, and better, more versatile gas grills have been developed. You will find in-depth information about gas grills in Chapter 1, as well as how they can be adapted to smoke-cooking in Chapter 2.

An entire chapter is devoted to smoke-cooking in *The Art of Grilling*. In it you will find information about charcoal-water smokers, step-by-step instructions for operating them, and techniques for getting great results. There are also guidelines for using your grill as a smoker. Over 40 new recipes for marinades, sauces, and relishes in Chapter 3 will expand your grilling repertoire with accompaniments that range from simple to complex. Chapter 4, "From Grill to Table," contains 24 all-new grill menus, each designed around a grilled main dish and one or two grilled side dishes.

The cooking times suggested in the recipes were arrived at using a kettle-shaped grill with mesquite charcoal. If you are cooking with a fuel other than mesquite charcoal, including gas, your times will be close but possibly a bit longer. Most kettle barbecues have a fuel grate and a cooking grid fixed 6 inches apart, so if your grill can be adjusted to bring the coals closer to the food this will reduce cooking time. The important rule to remember is don't worry. Check food periodically—it can always be returned to the grill to be cooked longer.

Charcoal grilling requires attention, but it also rewards with the pleasing sound of crackling coals, the aroma of wood smoke and food on the grill, and tender and juicy meals with that inimitable smoky flavor.

CHAPTER 1

TECHNIQUES & EQUIPMENT

TECHNIQUES & EQUIPMENT

The technique of cooking food over hot embers has existed for thousands of years. One of the earliest grilling methods was brought to this country by the Spanish from the Caribbean, where the native Indians wove a *barbacoa* lattice of green wood branches and cooked food on it over smoldering coals. French settlers in the South developed their own *barbe-a-queue* method of slow-roasting whole animals, literally cooking them from "whiskers to tail."

Nineteenth-century cattlemen adapted the idea of "barbecue" for cooking out on the range, discovering that slow-cooking tough slabs of meat and ribs with a basting sauce made the meat tender and delicious. From the North, American Indians passed along their technique of cooking with a combination of steam and hot embers. And the ancient tradition of preserving food by salting and smoking has evolved in these days of refrigeration into a delicious way of flavoring foods with the smoky taste of hardwood.

Though the techniques as well as the origins of these outdoor cooking methods overlap at many points, there are distinct differences.

GRILLING

Grilling is the quickest form of cooking over hot coals. The cooking time is under an hour, and the heat source is fairly close to the food. Foods for grilling should not need long, slow cooking. A marinade may be used for tenderizing, but the object of grilling is to quick-cook food to seal in moisture. It is by and large a dry-heat method of cooking, though basting can add flavor, and covering the grill can create moisture.

Open grilling is done without any cover over the grill. The coals remain hotter when the grill is open or uncovered, since the added air circulation promotes their burning. The cooking rack for open grilling is about 6 inches from the coals or closer, so that the heat is intense and undispersed and the food cooks quickly. *Searing* is done on an open grill. Food is cooked over high heat for a minute or so on each side as a way of quickly sealing in juices before further cooking at a lower temperature or with a cover or hood over the grill.

Covered grilling requires a vented cover or hood for the grill. Covering the grill makes it more ovenlike, since heat is reflected inside the grill, and food cooks more evenly. Moisture is released from the food and circulates inside the grill, keeping the food moist. With a cover on the grill you can control the intensity of the fire by opening the vents for more circulation or closing them down for a slower fire. Closing the vents completely will extinguish the fire.

Direct grilling is cooking directly over hot coals, whether the grill is open or covered. *Indirect* grilling, always done on a covered grill, is cooking food over a drip pan or water pan with the coals moved to the sides. If there is liquid in the water pan, steam is created, making for even moister cooking. The drip pan is most often used for fatty foods, such as duck or whole chicken, which need longer cooking without constant flare-ups. Indirect cooking is slower than direct, since the heat source is not directly under the food.

BARBECUING

Long, slow, smoky cooking over hardwood embers or charcoal with hardwood chunks describes barbecuing as we know it today. The regional variations in this country mainly spring from differences in the *sauce,* with each region stubbornly defending its own as the ultimate. These include the sweet tomato-based sauces of the deep South; the spicy sauces of Louisiana; the chili-pepper hot barbecue of Texas; the tangier, more vinegary sauces of the Southeast; Kansas City's sweet and spicy tomato sauce; and the Asian-influenced barbecue sauces of California. Home barbecuing can be done using indirect heat in a covered charcoal or gas grill or a smoker. Hardwood fuel or hardwood chunks mixed with charcoal to add flavor are essential. Keep the fire burning very low and add new charcoal every hour or so.

COLD-SMOKING AND SMOKE-COOKING

With *smokehouse smoking,* or *cold-smoking,* the food is away from direct heat and exposed only to the smoke. The temperature inside a cold smoker is very low—90° to 130°—not high enough to actually cook the food. The acids in the smoke act to preserve and dry the food. Food for cold-smoking first needs a brine soak, or "cure," that begins the process of preserving by drawing out moisture. After curing and cold-smoking, the food is still uncooked, and some foods will need additional cooking (such as bacon and some hams).

Smoke-cooking uses both heat and smoke to *cook* the food. The temperature is high enough—170° to 250°—to kill the growth of molds and bacteria, so curing is unnecessary. The food remains moist and tender, is deeply smoke-flavored, and is actually cooked at the end of the process rather than just preserved. Smoke-cooking is easier to do at home than cold-smoking, since it requires little attention and is a much faster process.

Smoke-cooking is done in a smoker, which looks like a tall kettle grill. Charcoal and gas grills can also be adapted to work like smokers with very good results, though a low, even temperature is harder to maintain and the heat source is closer to the food. See Chapter 2, "On Smoking," for more information on smoking.

CHARCOAL GRILLS

Nothing beats the delicious flavor of food cooked over real charcoal or hardwood. A hot fire seals in the natural juiciness of meats and poultry, and locks in the tenderness and moisture of fish and vegetables. Handling charcoal is somewhat more time-consuming than turning on a gas grill, and you do get your hands dirty, but in the long run, cooking with charcoal is more versatile and offers a wider range of flavors.

On the less tangible side in favor of charcoal grilling is the mystique of the fire, the crackle and hiss, the challenge of a heat source you can't measure. The wait for ready coals is enforced relaxation, since there is nothing else to do but let them burn down to the proper ash-covered state. Some don't enjoy this quirkiness, and would prefer a gas or electric grill. Since there are many options available, it is worth considering how you want to approach grilling before you invest in a grill.

As we mention in *Grill Book,* a well-made charcoal grill makes grilling easy and successful. The finish should be heat and rust resistant, such as enameled steel, stainless steel, or treated cast iron. Look for a grill supported by sturdy legs, with vents in the bottom and hood and a flat fuel grate (or firebox) for easier fire starting. An adjustable cooking rack is preferable, as is one made of rust-resistant materials. As obvious as it is that these elements make a good grill, it is a bit difficult to find them all in one product. Charcoal grill prices range from $10 up to $800, depending on features and durability. Contact the grill manufacturers listed in "Equipment Sources" at the end of this book for brochures and price lists to get a better idea of what is available if there are not many suppliers in your area.

Portable and Tabletop Grills: These grills, small enough to transport easily, are scaled-down versions of larger charcoal grills. The most often-seen portables are the hibachi and the Weber Smokey Joe, but there are many other varieties on the market. Some have covers, but most do not.

Braziers: Braziers, or open grills, are the least expensive and the least well made of the grills on the market. They lack a hood, so you are limited to open grilling, and extinguishing flare-ups is more difficult. Most braziers are unstable and made of flimsy materials, and often don't have vents in the bottom, which makes fire starting and fire control much harder. A wok cover or a makeshift cover of heavy-duty aluminum foil helps with flare-ups and temperature control.

Hooded Grills: These square or rectangular grills with hoods are often the best buy in charcoal grills, both for their versatility and good construction. Many of those available are made of solid, rustproof materials. They can offer more cooking flexibility, with adjustable cooking racks or firebox, grease catchers, warming racks, a charcoal door, and well-located vents. Hooded grills can be adapted for grilling, barbecuing, smoking, and ovenlike roasting. The price range for hooded grills is quite varied, from reasonable to very expensive.

Kettle Grills: The rounded kettle shape of this grill makes it more like an oven when closed, since the heat reflects evenly and circulates smoothly inside the grill. As an open grill a kettle is a little less versatile, since the fuel grate and cooking rack are fixed at 6 inches apart. A red-hot fire in a kettle grill, however, is hot enough for open grilling and searing. One disadvantage in some models is that the hood is not hinged onto the base, though most have a hook inside for hanging it on the side of the grill. The primary advantage of the kettle grill is the price, which is very reasonable given the quality of the manufacture.

Kamado: This Japanese cooker made of heavy earthenware is a grill, smoker, and oven in one. It is not as well suited to open grilling since the firebox is fixed at some distance from the cooking rack. It is designed primarily to be used with the heavy lid closed, so that the earthenware walls heat evenly and stay hot with amazingly little fuel. The kamado cooks evenly and keeps the food inside deliciously moist. It is expensive, but its versatility makes it worth it.

Fireplace Grills: These open grills are simply a cooking rack designed to be used over smoldering embers in a fireplace. For fireplace cooking, pull ashy, red-hot wood embers slightly forward in the fireplace and place the grill over them. Some fireplace grills are adjustable, but 4 to 6 inches of distance between the embers and the grill is desirable. Do *not* use charcoal in your fireplace.

Built-in Outdoor Grills: These cover quite a range of designs and uses. The most simple are set up for open grilling, and have just a firebox and cooking rack. More elaborate built-ins are designed for open or closed grilling and rotisserie, have an adjustable firebox with an access door, an adjustable cooking rack, a vented hood, and more. Keep these grills covered and rust free and you will get years of use from them.

About Fuels for Charcoal Grills

Use either hardwood burnt down to embers, hardwood charcoal, or briquets in charcoal grills. You can also mix charcoal with pieces of hardwood as a fuel supplement to give the food a smokier flavor, since charcoal alone burns virtually without smoke.

Start the dry hardwood chunks with the charcoal, and allow them to burn down with the coals to ashy red-hot embers before cooking. One note of caution: *Never* cook with charcoal inside your home or any enclosed space. Charcoal gives off enough carbon monoxide to be fatal. For grilling in your fireplace use only hardwood, *not* charcoal.

Hardwood: Use any hardwood, such as hickory, maple, ash, alder, oak, mesquite, cherry, apple, or the nut woods as fuel. Look for wood that has aged at least one year. Light a wood fire using kindling, not chemical starters. Allow the wood to burn

down and drop ashy embers before cooking. This may take 50 minutes to 1 hour. Do not use resinous softwoods such as pine, spruce, or cedar, which can contain pitch and give food a very unpleasant taste. Do not use plywood or lumber. These may have been treated with chemicals that could be toxic. As a general rule, do not use any wood you cannot identify.

Hardwood Charcoal or Lump Charcoal: Made from pure hardwood, this charcoal is clean burning and gives a subtle, pleasant smoky flavor to foods. It is made by smoldering hardwood chunks under controlled conditions until they become solid carbon charcoal. Hardwood charcoal burns, at its hottest, at about 800°, but at the gray-ash stage is an even 300° to 350°. Since there are no additives or filler to burn off, hardwood charcoal has a low ash content. It burns slowly and efficiently, and the coals won't need replenishing as often. It can be reused a second and sometimes a third time as a supplement to new charcoal. The second time around it lights more slowly, and without fresh charcoal it won't produce as hot a fire.

Mesquite Charcoal: Like hardwood charcoal, mesquite charcoal is made by converting mesquite hardwood to carbon chunks. It gets special mention here, however, because it behaves a bit differently than charcoal made from the other hardwoods. At its hottest it burns hotter—up to 1000°—than any other charcoal. It also spits and pops when it is first lit, sending out tiny hot charcoal shards, so always stand well away until the fireworks are over. Mesquite charcoal cooks quickly and cleanly, giving food a mild smoke flavor. It often comes in irregularly sized chunks, but these can be broken up with a hatchet if necessary. Mesquite charcoal can be reused a number of times, and burns efficiently with a low ash content. Mesquite is an excellent charcoal, reasonably priced and widely available.

Briquets: This ubiquitous grill fuel is unfortunately the cheapest, though its inefficiency makes it more costly than it appears. Briquets are made by carbonizing wood scraps and sawdust, combining them with filler and binder, and pressing the mixture into pillow-shaped squares. Briquets often contain a chemical additive for faster lighting, and some contain raw coal. Try to avoid those brands, since additives such as petroleum starter and coal will make food taste awful. There is also evidence that the chemical additives have a negative effect on the environment. Briquets must be completely coated with gray ash before cooking to allow any chemical additives and binders to burn off. At their hottest, briquets burn at about 600°, making them less effective for open grilling and searing. They do burn evenly, since they are designed to do so, though their overall temperature is lower than hardwood charcoals. They have a high ash content due to the fillers, so about one-quarter of the briquet drops into the ash pan without having provided much in the way of cooking heat, and the coals need to be replenished more often. Briquets are not reusable.

Lighting a Charcoal Fire

The watchwords of the charcoal fire are *plan ahead* and *be patient*. A charcoal fire, from the grill preparation to ready coals, requires a full 40 minutes. Start the grill well ahead of mealtime, taking into account both the start-up and the cooking times.

How Much Fuel?

A layer of coals 1½ to 2 coals deep and a little wider than the area needed for cooking should be enough charcoal for up to 1 hour. Only one layer of large hardwood coals is needed. Use the same number of coals for an indirect fire. When pushed to the sides the layers will then be up to 4 coals deep.

Fire-Starters

As we advise in *Grill Book* and strongly restate here, using kindling, a chimney, or an electric starter is a far better method of lighting charcoal than any of the chemical starters. Studies have also shown that the burn-off of chemical charcoal starters is damaging to the environment. Chimneys are widely available and relatively inexpensive given the amount of use you will get from one. There are two things to remember, however, if you *must* use flammable starters: *Never* squirt liquid starter on ignited coals. The stream will quickly become a river of fire up to your hand. Also, *never* use gasoline or kerosene, both of which can explode.

Kindling: Roll a sheet of newspaper on the diagonal and twist it into a loose, pretzel-shaped knot. Place this on the fuel grate and arrange plenty of dry twigs on top; place charcoal on top of the twigs. This is a simple kindling fire, and all that is required is lighting the paper (the newspaper step can be omitted if you have plenty of good kindling). Be sure that air can circulate freely around the twigs and charcoal, and that the bottom vents of the grill are open.

Chimney: This cylinder of perforated metal with a handle makes lighting a fire simple and fast (particularly if you live in an urban area where twigs are not that easy to come by). Place a loosely crumpled sheet of newspaper in the bottom, and pile the coals into the top three-quarters of the chimney. Open the hood and the vents in the bottom of the grill, remove the cooking rack, place the chimney on the fuel grate or firebox, and ignite the paper. If the coals are slow to light, add another crumpled sheet to the chimney after 2 or 3 minutes and re-ignite. When the coals at the top are well lit and the flaming has subsided, carefully dump the coals onto the grate or into the firebox. One disadvantage: You may find that the chimney doesn't hold as many coals as you need, particularly if you are using hardwood charcoal. Add new coals to the lit ones just after dumping them out and allow them to burn down to the desired temperature.

Electric Starter: This oval-shaped heating element is nestled among the coals piled on the fuel grate, with the vents and hood open. It is then plugged in to heat the coil, and in a short time the coals will be flaming. Remove the starter immediately when the coals in direct contact with the starter begin to glow, usually no more than 10 minutes. There are two disadvantages to the electric starter: a nearby electrical outlet is necessary, and for some this may not be available. Also, the starter initially lights only the coals it touches, so it takes a bit longer for the "starter" coals to ignite the rest.

Preparing the Cooking Rack

A rack coated with charred food bits gives the next meal cooked on it a bitter, stale flavor. Keep the cooking rack clean by scrubbing it with a stiff wire brush every time you cook (there are brushes designed specifically for this purpose, and a crum-

pled sheet of foil works well, also). The best rule of thumb is to scrape the rack immediately after cooking, while it is still warm. If you've been remiss, however, scrub the rack before putting it over the fire. Let it heat up over the fire and scrape it again.

Always preheat the cooking rack before cooking. This not only makes for more even cooking, but it gives food those characteristic grill marks.

You will need to oil the cooking rack occasionally to keep it seasoned, and to prevent food from sticking easily to the hot grill. Do this after the rack has been cleaned and has heated up. Using long-handled tongs, rub a small piece of cloth that has been saturated with oil over the rack, or use an old long-handled basting brush to apply oil. You can also use a chunk of fat trimmed from a piece of meat.

A Fire Ready for Cooking

Allow 30 to 45 minutes for a charcoal fire to be ready, slightly longer for a wood fire. The three stages of a cooking fire are described below. You can create a hotter fire by pushing the coals close together in a compact layer. For a slower fire, spread the coals out.

Red-hot Fire: If a red glow is visible through a thin coating of white ash, the coals are at their hottest, a red-hot fire. You will only be able to hold your palm over the fire for 3 seconds or so (at a distance of about 6 inches). This temperature is ideal for searing, and for quickly grilling non-fatty foods.

Medium-hot Fire: The coating of ash will be thicker and grayer and the red glow will be almost gone. You will be able to hold your palm over the fire for 5 to 7 seconds. For open grilling at this temperature, move the fire closer to the cooking rack. Otherwise, use a cover for the best results in cooking over a medium-hot fire.

Low Fire: The coating of gray ash is thick and there is no red glow. This temperature is ideal for slow-cooking foods on a covered grill.

Controlling the Heat and Managing Flare-ups

Opening the vents allows more air to circulate through the grill and heats up the coals. Contrarily, closing the vents by varying degrees will slow the fire. Move the coals close together for a hot fire; spread them out for a more moderate fire. To increase the heat of ashy coals, tap the coals with a long-handled tool to knock off the insulating ash.

Flare-ups are the bane of any griller. To avoid them from the start, make sure the fire has burned down enough to cook the foods you have selected. Cook fatty foods over a drip pan, or at the very least over a medium-hot to low fire. If you have found yourself faced with flare-ups despite your precautions, here are four suggestions:
• Move the food to a cooler part of the grill until the fire burns down a bit and is more manageable. Spread the coals out to cool the fire.
• Cover the grill and close the vents down by at least half, particularly the vents in the bottom, until the flare-ups have subsided and the fire has cooled down.
• Using a spray bottle with a well-directed stream, douse the flames *right at their source* with a squirt of water. Avoid overdoing it, or you may find you have no fire left at all. Spritzing can also displace ash, which may find its way to the surface of your food.
• Remove the food from the fire, close the vents down by over half to slow the fire, and wait until the fire is more manageable.

Cooking Times and Judging Doneness

The cooking times listed in this book are suggestions, since many outside factors can influence how long food needs to cook on the grill. Use a thermometer when recommended, and follow the visual checks given in the recipes to help you determine when food is done. Keep in mind these variables when calculating cooking time:
• Outside temperature, windiness, and humidity. Open grilling on a cool day will take longer than on a hot day. Wind makes the fire hotter; humidity makes the coals more sluggish.
• Temperature of the food before cooking. Bring food to room temperature to ensure more even cooking.

• Type of grill and distance of cooking rack from the fire. If your grill has an adjustable cooking rack, the time for open grilling will be shorter the closer the rack is to the fire. Covered cooking is faster on a kettle grill because heat is reflected more evenly inside.
• Type of fuel. Hardwood charcoal is hotter than briquets, and mesquite charcoal is even hotter. Bear in mind what fuel you are using when adjusting cooking times.
• Amount of food on the rack. If the food is packed together on the rack, the cooking time will be longer.

Adding Charcoal to a Fire

After approximately 1 hour of cooking you will need to add charcoal to the fire. Mesquite and hardwood charcoal *can* be added directly to the fire, though the crackling of mesquite may deposit little bits of charcoal on the food, and the fumes of lighting charcoal are not wholly desirable when cooking is in progress. The best way to add fuel is to light it in a chimney starter on a fireproof surface and add the glowing coals to the fire. This keeps the fire temperature even, and doesn't risk ashy bits on the food or give food an aftertaste.

Adding Smoke and Flavor to Charcoal Fires

For covered grilling, use untreated wood chips for adding a light smoky taste to foods, and wood chunks for more intense flavor. On an open grill, smoke will blow away and not flavor the food at all. Wood chips should be soaked in water for at least 30 minutes before adding them to the fire, and chunks need an hour. This produces a moist, flavorful smoke and keeps the small pieces from burning up too quickly. Place moist chips and chunks evenly over the coals, but don't overdo it as this may smother the fire. A handful or so of chips should be enough at one time, and 2 or 3 chunks of wood. Do not use resinous woods, plant clippings, or wood you can't identify. Do not use chips or chunks that have been treated or sprayed with chemicals. Those you buy specifically packaged for grilling will be free of chemicals. Wood chips and, to a lesser extent, wood chunks are most commonly available in these "flavors":

Hickory: The sweet, slightly spicy wood-smoke flavor of hickory is excellent for meats and poultry. It is a very versatile wood, available in both chips and chunks, and is the characteristic flavor generally associated with "smoked" food and barbecue.

Mesquite: Mesquite wood has an assertive but pleasant flavor, fine for meats, poultry, vegetables, and less delicately flavored fish. It is available in chips and chunks.

Alder: This is a somewhat mild smoke, but versatile. It is available in chips and usually chunks.

Nut Woods: Walnut and pecan wood give off a

mild but pleasant smoke flavor, suitable for meats and poultry. Available in chips only.

Fruit Woods: Cherry and apple are the most commonly available wood chips. Their flavor is mild but sweet—a nice wood smoke. The subtlety of fruit woods is best suited for pork, veal, poultry, and fish. These woods are seldom packaged in chunk form.

Dried Corncobs: Allow corncobs to dry out for a few days before using them. Their smoke has a hickorylike flavor.

Oak: The assertive, tangy smoke flavor of oak is best for beef. Oak is more often used for cooking rather than smoking.

Grapevine: The dried, tangly twigs and larger vine pieces of grapevine produce a delicate and subtly sweet smoke, excellent for poultry and fish.

Olive: Full flavored but not too strong, olive wood is an exotic smoke for meats and poultry.

Other Woods: You might also find sassafras, elder, beech, birch, or ash, among others. Experiment with the flavors, but avoid resinous woods, which give food an unpleasant taste.

In addition to wood chips and chunks, try dampened dried or fresh herb sprigs, fruit rinds, or unpeeled garlic cloves on the coals for subtle flavoring. Place them on the fire just before cooking, and cover the grill to get the full benefit of their odors.

Storing Charcoal

Charcoal's worst enemy is moisture, and leaving it in its original paper bag makes it very vulnerable. A large plastic garbage can with a tight-fitting lid is the ideal storage container for charcoal. It will hold as much as 40 pounds, and the wide opening makes it easy to select the size of chunks you want if you are cooking with hardwood or mesquite charcoal.

Shutting Down a Charcoal Grill

Close all the vents and cover the grill tightly to extinguish coals. If you get in the habit of doing this immediately after cooking, you will find that hardwood charcoal can be reused at least once. Extinguish an open grill fire by dousing it lightly with water. Check it half an hour later to make sure the coals have completely gone out.

Keeping the Charcoal Grill Clean

Regularly dump the ashes. The outside of your grill can be cleaned with warm sudsy water. It is not necessary to clean the inside of your grill, though if you'd like to clean it use a foaming oven cleaner. Spray it on, leave it long enough to soften the grease, and wipe it out with paper towels. Keep the grill out of bad weather if possible, and cover it with a plastic cover.

GAS GRILLS

If it is more appealing to you to run out to the back-yard, turn a knob and punch a button, and have a ready grill in about 15 minutes—all without getting your hands dirty—then a gas grill is for you. The distinctive smoky flavor of charcoal won't be there. Gas grills depend on the smoke produced by fat dripping on the lava rocks to give food a grilled flavor, but there are ways of creating a smokier flavor on a gas grill. And gas grills, once you are past the initial investment, are cheaper to cook on than charcoal grills. The gas tank typically holds 5 gallons (or 20 pounds) of fuel, and needs refilling after 24 total cooking hours (measured at the highest setting, so fuel lasts considerably longer cooking at medium or low). Liquid propane fuel can be found at some gas stations, RV centers, or U-Haul rental centers, and a refill costs $6 to $8.

Gas grills are all of one general design. Their heat source is from burners fueled either by liquid propane or natural gas, over which a bed of lava rocks is positioned to evenly distribute the heat (some newer grills have bars that heat up, rather than rocks). Above the rocks is a cooking rack (or two) and a hinged hood. Natural gas grills are permanently installed and hooked up to an underground gas line. LP grills are usually built into a moveable cart.

What to Look for in a Gas Grill

As with a charcoal grill, sturdy construction of rustproof materials is a must. Look for temperature controls designed to stay cool—either away from the heat or shielded. Fuel tanks should be easy to change. The ignition button should light the gas jets in one or two tries. Test these features at the dealership. Two-burner models give you more versatility, since one side can be at a different setting.

Lighting a Gas Grill

Follow the manufacturer's instructions for your grill. Always turn your face away from the grill when igniting it, since the temperature setting will probably be on high and the burners may catch very suddenly. Allowing the gas to run without immediately igniting the burner can cause a dangerous build-up of gas that will flash when lit. If the ignition doesn't work immediately, turn off the gas, allow it to dissipate, and start over, this time with a long match for manually lighting the burners (consult the manufacturer's instructions for match-lighting).

For most gas grills the procedure is as follows:
• *Open the hood.* Do not fail to follow this *very* important step.
• Open the gas tank valve.
• Turn the temperature control knob to high. On two-burner grills turn on the right-hand side only.
• Turn your face away from the open grill and immediately press the ignition button. The burner should light with one or two tries.
• Turn the left-hand burner knob to high; the right side will ignite the left.

Preheating the Grill and Controlling the Temperature

Gas grills need to be preheated so that the cooking rack is hot enough for searing and the lava rocks evenly heated for efficient cooking. Preheat grills on the highest setting for a minimum of 15 minutes. If you are searing the food, sear on high, reduce the heat immediately to the medium setting, and continue to cook at that temperature or lower. The lava rocks heat and will continue to cook food, even when the grill is off, so experiment with different temperature settings.

On high, gas grills reach temperatures up to 700°, equivalent to a red-hot briquet or hardwood charcoal fire. Gas grills cook most evenly and with the fewest flare-ups at medium or low, with temperatures in the 250° to 400° range, roughly the same as medium-hot to low for charcoal. Quick-cooking foods can be grilled at the highest or medium setting, and slow-cooking, fatty foods, and warming can be done at low or even off, so that the heated lava rocks do the cooking.

Preparing the Cooking Racks

To prepare for cooking the next time, scrub the cooking rack well with a wire brush while the grill is warm after you've finished cooking. This keeps the grease from hardening on the rack. If you forgot to clean the rack the last time you cooked, scrub it once with a wire brush, preheat the grill, and scrub it again before cooking.

To prevent food from sticking to the cooking rack, soak a small rag with cooking oil and coat the rack, holding the rag with long-handled tongs. You can also use an old long-handled basting brush dipped in oil, or a chunk of fat cut from a piece of meat, held in long-handled tongs.

Managing Flare-ups

Do not squirt water on a gas grill to extinguish flare-ups. All gas grills have hoods, and by closing the hood and turning the heat down you can successfully manage any flare-ups. Remove the food from the grill, if necessary. Trim as much fat from fatty foods as possible, or position a drip pan on top of the lava rocks and under the food if necessary.

Cooking Times and Judging Doneness

See the paragraph of the same name in the Charcoal Grill section of this chapter, page 20.

Adding Smoke and Flavor to Gas Grills

Most gas grill manufacturers advise against putting wood chips and chunks directly on the lava rocks or burners, since the ash can clog the gas lines and become dangerous. A successful alternative is to place a foil "log" or disposable aluminum pan containing wood chips on top of the lava rocks.

Use untreated hardwood chips. Soak them for at least 30 minutes before cooking. For cooking longer than 1 hour, soak enough chips to make several logs. Tear off a foot-long piece of heavy-duty aluminum foil and fold it in half lengthwise. Sprinkle several handfuls of dampened chips down the middle. Crimp the long sides together along the top, and loosely turn up the ends to keep the chips from falling out. You should have a long rectangular "log." Poke holes in the log to let the smoke escape. Place it directly on the lava rocks and pre-

heat it while preheating the grill. The chips should begin to smoke soon after you start cooking. If you are using a disposable aluminum pan, poke holes in the bottom of it, put several handfuls of chips in the pan, and place it directly on the rocks. Preheat it with the grill.

For information on the various types of wood chips and chunks, see the paragraph entitled "Adding Smoke and Flavor to Charcoal Fires" in the Charcoal Grill section of this chapter, page 20.

Cleaning a Gas Grill

Follow the manufacturer's instructions for cleaning your gas grill, including the lava rocks, burners, and gas tubes. Preheating the grill will usually burn off old grease from earlier cooking, but occasionally a more thorough cleaning is recommended. Replace the lava rocks when necessary.

ELECTRIC GRILLS

Electric grills, though clean and easy to maintain, least resemble the traditional charcoal grill. They are more like a broiler with the heating element underneath rather than above, and food to be cooked on them should be basted or marinated to give it full flavor. Some electric grills have lava rocks or iron stones to create some smoke from dripping fat, but they are by and large smoke-free. They generally do not have hoods, so flat cuts of meat, poultry, fish, and vegetables are best for electric grills: foods that cook quickly and require no ambient heat. Consult the manufacturer's instructions for the best ways to use your electric grill.

Electric grills do have the advantage of being safe for use indoors. They are also suited for apartment and condo decks where open fires and flare-ups are not acceptable.

Keep the cooking rack clean; most can be removed and washed in soapy water. Oil the cooking rack before cooking to keep food from sticking. Preheat the rack to sear the food and give it grill marks.

TOOLS AND TIPS

In *Grill Book* we describe a number of tools, some that are basic to grilling, and others that expand your grilling style. We will repeat many of those tools here, and add several that are new on the market or are home-grill inspirations, all designed for making grilling easier.

Heavy-duty Mitts: Always have one or more of these nearby.

Long-handled Tongs: The spring-loaded variety are the easiest to operate. Use them for moving everything from coals to food.

Charcoal Starter: If you are not using kindling for your charcoal fire, invest in either a charcoal chimney or an electric starter. Avoid chemical starters and lighter-impregnated charcoal.

Wire Grill Brush: Every conscientious griller will have one of these for cleaning the cooking rack.

Heavy-duty Aluminum Foil: This handy substance is excellent for a number of chores:
• For grilling fragile fish or food that could fall through the cooking rack, poke holes in a sheet of foil and grill on it rather than directly on the rack.
• Crumple it and scrape the rack as a makeshift grill brush.
• Fold it into logs and fill with wood chips for gas-grill smoke.
• Line the firebox for easier ash clean-up.
• Line the water pan in a charcoal-water smoker for easier clean-up.

Skewers: Great for grilling vegetables, small items, and kebabs. Soak wood skewers for at least 15 minutes; metal skewers should be notched or twisted to keep food from spinning around as you turn them on the grill.

Basting Brushes: Look for the long-handled variety for safety.

Spatulas or Turners: Long-handled, bent-bladed spatulas are ideal for the grill.

Marinade Pans: Glass, porcelain or enamel, stainless steel, disposable shiny aluminum, or ceramic are best. Avoid uncoated aluminum pans, which tend to react with acidic marinades.

Drip Pans: Disposable aluminum pans are easy to use and can be thrown away after cooking.

Spray Bottle: It's a good thing to have on hand, though you will want to try other means of extinguishing flare-ups before resorting to it.

Flashlight: Handy for grilling in the dark.

Thermometer: There is nothing like a good-quality instant-reading thermometer for judging doneness.

Grill Thermometer: If you are concerned about the internal temperature of your covered grill, use an inexpensive oven thermometer or a thermometer with a magnetic back designed specifically for the grill.

LP Gas Gauge: Buy one that fits your LP tank valve. If the manufacturer doesn't sell one, look for a gauge that attaches to the outside of the tank and indicates the level of gas remaining.

Extra LP Gas Tank: To be certain you will never run out of gas in the middle of cooking, buy an extra tank and keep it filled.

Hinged Wire Grill Baskets: These baskets hold the food between two wire racks, and the whole unit is placed on the grill. Hinged grill baskets are particularly well suited for whole fish and fish fillets, as well as for food too small for the cooking rack. They come in a variety of shapes and sizes. Oil the inside of the baskets before cooking to keep food from sticking.

Knives and Carving Board: Good sharp knives help cut into food for judging doneness; a carving board with a juice catcher saves those delicious juices.

CHAPTER 2

ON SMOKE-COOKING FOODS

ON SMOKE-COOKING FOODS

Smoking foods originated as a means of preservation long before the development of refrigeration and canning. Food was first cured in a salt brine and then smoked at very low temperatures for long periods, a process that removed moisture and changed texture. Some foods would then still require cooking, since this type of smoking was only meant for preserving. The result was often rather salty, but the food had a delicious deeply smoked flavor. This technique of cold-smoking at temperatures between 90° and 120° still exists, though a smokehouse or a cold smoker with carefully controlled conditions is needed for producing the characteristic Virginia hams and country-style bacons.

Smoke-cooking is a method of giving food a rich, smoky flavor while cooking it at the same time, a technique much better suited to the equipment available to the home griller. The temperature inside the smoker is high enough to kill the growth of molds and bacteria, thus brining the foods in advance is unnecessary. The food is penetrated with flavor from the combination of hardwood smoke and steam, and the moisture keeps the foods tender and juicy. Smoke-cooking is much faster than cold-smoking, and constant vigilance is not necessary as in grilling. Smoke-cooked food is less salty than cold-smoked food, and is fully cooked after smoking.

ABOUT SMOKERS

There are a number of different kinds of smokers on the market, designed specifically for smoking foods. The most widely available are smoke-cookers or charcoal-water smokers, which cook the food with heat, smoke, and steam. There are also cold-smokers designed to simulate the smokehouse effect of smoking at very low temperatures. Since it is necessary to maintain the temperature in this type of smoker over a very long period of time, most of them run on gas or electricity, and have thermostats. They have a heat source, a pan for wood chips, and racks for holding the food. Follow the manufacturer's instructions for operating gas and electric smokers. The focus of this chapter, however, is on smoke-cooking rather than cold-smoking.

Look for sturdy, solid construction in a smoker; if it is on legs, make certain they are very stable so the smoker can't be tipped over. The materials should be rustproof, and the cooking rack nickel-plated. Check to make sure the vents move easily.

Charcoal-Water Smokers

The design for these smokers is generally standard: a firebox or fuel grate in the bottom, a water pan suspended over the charcoal, one or two cooking racks over the water pan, and a hood. The adjustable vents keep the charcoal at the desired temperature while creating maximum smoke inside. A door in the side for adding charcoal is an absolute must. Because of the number of levels in a smoker, most are tall and either square or cylindrical, like an elongated kettle barbecue. Charcoal must be added to the charcoal-water smoker every hour or so, and smoke flavor is created by adding dampened wood chunks.

The *kamado* is a unique Japanese cooker made of very heavy earthenware. It is a smoker as well as an oven and barbecue. It requires very little fuel, since the earthenware walls become hot and retain heat very efficiently. A water pan is not necessary for smoking in the kamado; the smoking process is more like slow roasting than smoke-cooking, and the moisture from the food provides the steam. Do not use charcoal with any additives in a kamado, or any chemical fire-starters.

Gas and Electric Smokers

There are gas and electric smokers designed like the charcoal water smoker, except that the heat source is typically lava rocks heated by either a gas burner or an electric element, and you need a foil log filled with wood chips to create smoke. They require less attention than charcoal smokers, and the inside temperature is consistent and often adjustable, but the smoke is not as ample from chips as it is from wood chunks burning on a charcoal fire.

HOW TO SMOKE-COOK

The following directions apply to an elongated kettle-shaped charcoal-water smoker. Check the manufacturer's instructions for more details about the operation of your particular smoker.

How to Light a Charcoal Smoker

• Begin soaking up to 8 hardwood chunks in water (see the "Smoking Time Guide" at the end of this chapter for the suggested number of wood chunks).
• Remove the hood, cooking racks, water pan, and the middle section of the smoker if it is detachable. Remove the charcoal ring if your smoker has one.
• Open all the vents.
• Using a charcoal chimney, kindling, or an electric starter, light enough coals on the fuel grate for a 2-coal-deep layer (some shorter-cooking foods will require fewer coals. This is indicated in the "Smoking Time Guide"). See Chapter 1, page 17, for more on starting a charcoal fire. Do not use treated briquets or chemical starters. The coals will be ready in 30 to 40 minutes, or when they are covered with gray ash. Replace the charcoal ring (if applicable) and spread the coals evenly over the fuel grate.
• Put the middle section of the smoker onto the bottom section (if this applies to your smoker).
• Line the inside and out of the water pan with heavy-duty aluminum foil to make future clean-up easier (this step is optional).
• Place the water pan in position and carefully fill it nearly to the top with hot liquid. Do not try to put the pan in place with liquid in it.
• Put the lower cooking rack in place and arrange the food on it in a single layer. Do not crowd the food. Bear in mind that the food above will drip down on what is below, so make sure the flavors are compatible. Also, place longer-cooking food on the lower rack so that the food on top can be removed with a minimum of disruption.
• Put the top cooking rack in place and arrange the food on it.
• Cover the smoker and close all the vents by one-third (vents may be adjusted later, depending on the internal temperature of the smoker). Use a mitt to protect your hands when adjusting the vents.

• Put 3 or 4 damp wood chunks on the coals through the charcoal door, using a mitt and long-handled tongs.
• Disturb the smoker as little as possible while cooking.

Adding Wood Chunks

Wood chunks should be soaked for at least 1 hour before adding them to the smoker. Shake off excess water before putting them on the coals, and distribute them well to avoid snuffing out any section of the fire. Use long-handled tongs and a mitt for adding wood chunks. As a general rule, start out with no more than 4 wood chunks. When these have burned off, usually after a few hours, add more wood if desired. The more wood chunks you add, the more heavily smoked the food will be.

Maintaining the Temperature Inside the Smoker

Smoke-cooking is done at temperatures between 170° and 250°. The technique to master in smoking, therefore, is keeping the smoker in that range.

Some smokers have a temperature gauge built into the hood, but most gauges are not reliable and usually give out in short order. It is best not to rely on them. An instant-reading thermometer dropped into the top vent (if your smoker has one) is a fairly accurate method of reading the inside temperature, but not foolproof. Instant-reading thermometers are designed to be inserted into food, and have a tendency to read low when measuring air temperature. The most reliable way to check the temperature is to put an oven thermometer inside the smoker and check it from time to time. The drawback here, of course, is that the smoker must be opened, and this will extend the cooking time. The best solution is to go without a thermometer (or use one for the first few times you smoke to get the hang of your equipment).

Some general guidelines for checking and maintaining the temperature inside the smoker are:
• If you can put your hand on the hood of the smoker and leave it there fairly comfortably for a second or two, the smoker is hot enough but not too hot. If it is cool enough to leave your hand on it for an extended period, the smoker is too cool.

- The vents on the bottom should never be completely closed. If the fire is too hot, close them down a bit. If too cool, open them all the way.
- The oxygen provided by opening the charcoal door will revive the coals. Tap the coals with long-handled tongs to knock off some of the heavy ash, if necessary.
- Don't allow the charcoal in the smoker to die out before adding more.
- Avoid opening the hood of the smoker. The smoker cooks more evenly if left largely undisturbed.

Adding Coals

Add coals every 1 to 1½ hours. You can add unlit hardwood charcoal directly to the smoker, but as it ignites it gives off fumes that may affect the flavor of the food. For best results, light the charcoal in a charcoal chimney on a heatproof surface and add hot coals to the smoker with long-handled tongs. This also serves to keep the smoker at a more even temperature.

Adding to the Water Pan

The water pan should always be at least half full for smoke-cooking. You may need to add more liquid after about 4 hours of smoking, which can be done through the charcoal door. Heat the liquid before adding it.

Using Your Charcoal and Gas Grill as a Smoker

Your barbecue grill can be adapted to smoke foods as long as it has a tight-fitting hood with plenty of space inside for smoke to circulate. The cooking time will be somewhat shorter, so check doneness with an instant-reading thermometer.

In a charcoal grill, light the coals in the fuel grate. When completely covered with gray ash, move them to one side of the fuel grate. Place a disposable aluminum water pan on the other side of the grate and half fill it with heated smoking liquid (water, or one of the alternatives discussed on page 33). Make a loose foil log filled with dampened wood chips and poke it with holes (see page 23). Place it on the coals. Replace the cooking rack, arrange the food on the grill over the water pan, and cover the grill. Keep the vents partially closed, and replenish

the coals every hour or so. Add more liquid and chips as needed.

A gas grill can also be adapted for smoke-cooking. Place a disposable aluminum water pan on one side of the grill, directly on the lava rocks. Fill it half full with smoking liquid. On the other side, directly on the lava rocks, place a loose foil log filled with dampened wood chips (see page 23). Preheat the grill on high, and when the water is hot and the chips are smoking, arrange the food on the cooking rack and cover the grill. Turn the heat to low. Add more liquid and chips as needed. If your grill has two burners, turn the heat off under the water pan and turn the other burner to low.

FUEL AND SMOKE FLAVORINGS

Many things come together to produce the smoky flavor in a charcoal-water smoker. The fuel you use, the wood you have selected for smoking, the liquid and flavorings in the water pan, and any marinade or rub on the food will all contribute something to the final outcome, so try to match the appropriate flavors with the food. One rule of thumb: When smoke-cooking, your flavor choices can never be too simple, since even the most basic combination of charcoal, wood chunks, and water in the water pan will give you a delicious, flavorful result. It is possible to overdo by using a strong wood smoke or an assertive steaming liquid with delicate foods.

Smoker Fuel

Charcoal is the best fuel for smokers, since hardwood is difficult to light quickly for replenishing the fire and burns out more quickly. You will be using hardwood chunks, however, so you will still have the advantages of flavorful wood smoke. Within the world of charcoal there are some differences that you will want to consider before smoking. See Chapter 1, "About Fuels for Charcoal Grills" on page 16, for more detailed information about charcoal.

Hardwood Charcoal or Lump Charcoal: Carbonized hardwood burns cleanly and relatively evenly, and gives food a light, pleasant smoky flavor. It burns longer and hotter than briquets, and not quite as hot as mesquite. It is an excellent fuel for smoking.

Mesquite Charcoal: Mesquite burns very cleanly though somewhat less evenly than other hardwood charcoal. It tends to burn hotter than other hardwoods, so the vents will need to be adjusted accordingly. It is a very good fuel for smoking, though a bit tricky to manage. It is the least expensive hardwood charcoal.

Briquets: Briquets are designed to burn evenly, are easy to start, and burn at a temperature well suited to smoking. They do, however, burn up more quickly than hardwood charcoal, and do not cook as cleanly since they contain fillers. Do not use briquets that have chemical additives, and do not light them with liquid starter. If you are adding briquets during the smoking process, they must be lit outside the smoker and then added, since the fillers in briquets can give off unpleasant fumes when igniting. Briquets are a good fuel for smoking, but look for a brand with the fewest additives.

Wood Chunks and Chips

The most effective way to add smoke in a charcoal-water smoker is to use hardwood chunks that have been soaked in water for at least 1 hour. Chunks are about 2 by 3 inches, and burn much longer than chips. Usually, a maximum of 6 chunks are sufficient to smoke foods for up to 8 hours. For a heavier smoke flavor or longer smoking time, more can be used. Unfortunately, many wood chunk distributors have limited the "flavors" they market. The most commonly available chunks are hickory and mesquite. Green logs can be used without presoaking.

Dampened chips can be wrapped in a loose foil log (see page 23) and placed directly on the coals. They can also be tossed directly onto the fire, but they burn up more quickly. Since chips are available in a wider variety of woods, you can augment the smoke from wood chunks with an occasional handful of wood chips of a different flavor. Do not use softwoods such as pine, fir, or cedar. Do not use lumber or plant clippings, any wood you can't identify, or wood that has been treated with chemicals. See Chapter 1, "Adding Smoke and Flavor to Charcoal Fires" on page 20, for more information on hardwood chunks and chips.

Hickory is an excellent hardwood for smoking. Its sweet, spicy flavor is compatible with every type of food. The distinctive but not-too-strong flavor of *mesquite* is also compatible with all foods. *Oak* has an assertive smoke best for beef. The smoke from *dried corncobs* is reminiscent of hickory wood. The *nut woods* and *fruit woods* such as pecan, walnut, cherry, and apple are excellent for smoking delicate foods, but are hard to find in chunk form. *Grapevine* offers a subtle, delicate flavor. *Alder* smoke combines well with most foods.

Filling the Water Pan

The liquid and aromatics in the water pan mingle with the hardwood smoke to tenderize food and give it flavor. Try to match the vapor and smoke to the food you are cooking, to add flavor without overpowering delicate food. Always add hot liquid to the pan. It should be one-half to three-quarters water, supplementing the rest with the flavoring liquid of your choice.

Water: Water is the vehicle for pure hardwood smoke.

Wine: White wine flavors delicately, and can be used with poultry, fish, and vegetables. Red wine has a more assertive flavor, and is better with beef, pork, or lamb.

Beer: Beer creates a nice, sweet smoky vapor that combines well with most foods.

Stock: Use a stock compatible with the food you are smoking. It gives a mild, pleasant flavor.

Citrus Juice: Use in small amounts for poultry, fish, and vegetables.

Spirits: Use in small amounts for beef, pork, and lamb.

Adding aromatics to the liquid in the water pan will also subtly flavor the food. Some suggestions are:
- Fresh or dried chilies
- Peeled garlic cloves
- Fresh or dried herbs
- Spices
- Citrus peels or citrus halves or slices
- Fresh ginger

Marinades for Smoking

Food destined for the charcoal-water smoker do not need to be marinated, since the steam from the water pan tenderizes tough foods. If pure smoke flavor is the desired objective, you can simply rub the food with a little oil. In addition to an oil rub try seasoning the food inside and out, putting aromatics in the cavities of poultry or fish, or rubbing the outside with garlic. Sometimes the simple approach is best.

Marinades do, however, tenderize meats and add flavor. Bastes flavor the outside of the food at the end of cooking and give the food an attractive exterior. Baste foods in a smoker only toward the end of cooking, and add an extra half an hour to an hour to make up for the times you open the smoker. Marinate foods in nonreactive containers such as glass, porcelain, ceramic, stainless steel, or enamel. Avoid uncoated aluminum.

Brines or cures are not necessary for cooking food in a water smoker, since it will cook at a high enough temperature to ward off bacteria and mold, and the food will be *cooked* rather than *preserved*.

Try any of the marinades in Chapter 3 or use the flavor-infused oils as bastes (page 45); the Molasses and Bourbon Glaze (page 48), Bourbon Barbecue Sauce (page 48), and Asian-style Barbecue Sauce (page 49) are also excellent for basting on the food as it smokes.

Taking Care of the Smoker

Regularly dump the ashes from your smoker. Clean the cooking racks each time after you use the smoker—don't let the grease build up. Do this by scraping the racks well with a grill brush and, if necessary, cleaning them in the sink in soapy water. The outside of the smoker can be cleaned with warm sudsy water or spray-on cleaner. Do not use abrasive cleaners on the finish. The water pan may be cleaned with spray-on oven cleaner, but cleaning the inside walls or hood of the smoker is not necessary or desirable. Keep your smoker covered, and out of bad weather if possible.

Using Smoked Foods

Smoked foods are delicious served cold, and since they will last in the refrigerator for up to 2 weeks, it makes sense to cook extra when you smoke. Smoked fish, chicken, duck, turkey, and game birds make delicious salads. These are also excellent sliced for sandwiches. Smoked meats can be reheated for hot sandwiches, or served cold.

Tips for Safety and Success

• Do not use a smoker indoors or in an enclosed space.
• Avoid using the smoker on a windy day.
• Set up the smoker away from the house or eaves. Make sure it is positioned so that the smoke does not blow into an open window (including your neighbor's!).
• Set up the smoker on level ground on a heatproof surface. A wood deck is not a wise location for a smoker.
• Do not use chemically treated briquets or liquid starter in a smoker.
• Keep children and pets away from a hot smoker.
• Avoid opening the smoker if possible, to maintain even heat and achieve better results.
• Use mitts when handling the hot smoker and vents.
• To extinguish the fire, replace the hood and close all the vents completely. Do not douse the fire with water.
• Keep the smoker clean.

Smoking Time Guide

This cooking chart is based on cooking in a charcoal-water smoker. Many variables can affect the smoking time, so don't try to set up the meal for split-second timing, and use these times as a *guide* rather than gospel. An instant-reading thermometer is a good tool to use together with the suggested cooking times. Insert the thermometer into the thickest part of the food, but not touching the bone. Some variables to keep in mind for smoking are:

- Outside temperature, wind, and humidity. Wind will heat the coals more quickly; some vent adjustment may be necessary, and charcoal may need to be added more frequently. Food will cook more slowly on a cold day. Humidity can make the coals sluggish.
- Bring the food to room temperature before smoking. If you haven't done so, add extra cooking time.
- Hardwood charcoal burns a little hotter than briquets, and lasts a little longer.
- Open the smoker as seldom as possible while cooking. Add extra time if you have opened it several times.
- Add new charcoal before the coals in the smoker get too low. This helps keep the temperature even.

- Add new charcoal before the coals in the smoker get too low. This helps keep the temperature even.

BEEF	Weight or Thickness	Charcoal	Wood Chunks	Cooking Time	Doneness in Fahrenheit
Roasts	3 to 5 pounds	2 layers	4 to 6	4 to 5 hours	135° rare 150° medium 170° well
Brisket	5 to 7 pounds	2 layers	4 to 6	4 to 6 hours	160° to 170° well
Ribs	2 to 3 inches	2 layers	4 to 6	3 to 4 hours	160° to 170° well
PORK					
Roasts	3 to 5 pounds	2 layers	4 to 6	4 to 6 hours	155° to 165° juicy
Chops	1¼ inches	2 layers	4 to 6	2 to 3 hours	155° to 165° juicy
Ribs	Full slab	2 layers	4 to 6	3 to 5 hours	meat begins to pull away from bone
Ribs	Country-style	2 layers	4 to 6	4 to 6 hours	meat begins to pull away from bone
Ham	10 to 14 pounds	2 layers	3 to 4	3 to 4 hours	140° heated through
Sausage	1-inch thick	1 layer	2 to 4	2 to 3 hours	155° to 165° juicy
LAMB					
Roasts	5 to 7 pounds	2 layers	4 to 6	4 to 6 hours	140° to 160° medium
Leg	5 to 7 pounds	2 layers	4 to 6	4 to 6 hours	140° to 160° medium
Chops	1¼ inches	1 layer	3 to 4	2 to 3 hours	140° medium
POULTRY					
Chicken	Cut up	1 layer	2 to 4	3 to 4 hours	160° to 170° juicy
Chicken, whole	3 to 4 pounds	2 layers	3 to 5	4 to 5 hours	160° to 170° juicy
Chicken, whole	5+ pounds	2 layers	4 to 6	5 to 6 hours	160° to 170° juicy
Turkey, whole, unstuffed	8 to 12 pounds	2 layers	5 to 7	7 to 8 hours	160° to 170° juicy
Turkey, whole unstuffed	13 to 18 pounds	2 layers	6 to 8	9 to 11 hours	160° to 170° juicy
Turkey, bone-in breast	5 to 7 pounds	2 layers	3 to 5	5 to 7 hours	160° to 165° juicy
Duck	4 to 6 pounds	2 layers	3 to 5	4 to 6 hours	160° juicy
Cornish game hen	1½ pounds	1 layer	2 to 3	3 to 4 hours	160° to 170° juicy

FISH	Weight or Thickness	Charcoal	Wood Chunks	Cooking Time	Doneness in Fahrenheit
Large whole	4 to 6 pounds	1 layer	3 to 5	3 to 4 hours	Flakes with a fork
Small whole	Up to 2 pounds	1 layer	2 to 3	1 to 2 hours	Flakes with a fork
Fillets, Steaks	1½ inches	1 layer	2 to 3	1 to 2 hours	Flakes with a fork
Shellfish		1 layer	2 to 3	1 to 2 hours	Firm
GAME					
Venison	5 to 7 pounds	2 layers	4 to 6	4 to 6 hours	170° well
Pheasant	3 to 5 pounds	2 layers	4 to 6	4 to 6 hours	160° to 170°
Goose	8 to 10 pounds	2 layers	4 to 6	7 to 8 hours	170° juicy
Small game birds	¾ to 2 pounds	1 layer	2 to 4	2 to 4 hours	Leg moves easily
VEGETABLES					
Eggplant	Slices	1 layer	2 to 3	1 to 2 hours	Tender when pierced with a skewer
Onion	Whole	1 layer	2 to 3	2 to 3 hours	Tender
Bell peppers	Whole	1 layer	2 to 3	1 to 2 hours	Tender
Tomato	Whole	1 layer	2 to 3	½ to 1 hour	Soft
Winter squash	Slices	1 layer	2 to 3	2 to 3 hours	Tender
Summer squash	Whole	1 layer	2 to 3	1 to 2 hours	Tender
Garlic	Whole head	1 layer	2 to 3	2 to 3 hours	Soft

CHAPTER 3

MARINADES, SAUCES, & RELISHES

MARINADES, SAUCES, & RELISHES

With a little practice, the right marinade, baste, or sauce can give your dish either a subtle sweetness or tang, pack a spicy punch, or transform a tough cut of meat into a tender and juicy meal. Acidic marinades are for tenderizing and flavoring meats, and need several hours to do so. Oil marinades add moisture to lean food, keep it from sticking to the grill, and give it a crisp and flavorful skin. Paste marinades give food a savory crust, and a more penetrating flavor if allowed to marinate for several hours. Seasonings and bastes give food a burst of flavor on the outside, while sauces and relishes are served as complements to the food after it is cooked.

Some marinating rules of thumb:
• Marinate meats for 2 hours at room temperature, or longer in the refrigerator.
• Marinate poultry for 2 hours at room temperature, or longer in the refrigerator.
• Marinate vegetables and fish at room temperature for 30 minutes, or 2 hours maximum in the refrigerator.
• Remove food from the refrigerator 30 minutes before grilling to bring it to room temperature. Food will cook more evenly if it starts at room temperature.
• Salt generally is not called for in most marinades, since it draws the juices out of uncooked meat. Salt only after food is grilled—you may find that the smoky grill flavor is a good salt substitute.
• Use glass, enamel, porcelain, coated aluminum, or stainless steel bowls, dishes, and pans for marinating. Avoid uncoated aluminum and plastic (plastic absorbs odors).

ACIDIC MARINADES

Acidic marinades contain wine, vinegar, soy sauce, mustard, citrus juice, or yogurt, which acts on food with tough fibers, breaking it down and tenderizing it. Meats can marinate in acidic marinades for 2 hours or longer. Acidic marinades are also used for flavoring, since the acidic element will penetrate the food. Meat needs a minimum of 2 hours

for any flavor to penetrate it, and poultry 2 hours or longer, if desired. Vegetables and fish only need 30 minutes or so at room temperature, and 2 hours in the refrigerator. Use plenty of aromatics (such as fresh herbs) in acidic marinades for flavor, and a little oil to keep the food from drying out on the grill.

WHITE WINE MARINADE   *2 cups*

This is a basic marinade for poultry, oily fish, shellfish, and vegetables. Use an aromatic of your choice, or a combination.

> **1½ cups dry white wine**
> **¼ cup olive oil**
> **1 small onion, sliced**
> **1 small carrot, sliced into coins**
> **Several large pieces fresh lemon peel**
> **1 heaping tablespoon chopped fresh herb leaves, such as tarragon, basil, sage, oregano, or rosemary, or 1 teaspoon dried herbs**
> **1 teaspoon black peppercorns, crushed**

Combine all the ingredients. Marinate poultry for up to 2 hours at room temperature, or longer in the refrigerator. Marinate vegetables, fish, and shellfish for up to 30 minutes at room temperature, or 2 hours in the refrigerator.

RED WINE MARINADE   *2 cups*

This basic marinade is best for meats of all kinds, particularly those that need some tenderizing. Try varying the wine to vary the flavor. For larger roasts, double the recipe.

> **1½ cups dry red wine**
> **¼ cup olive oil**
> **1 small onion, sliced**
> **1 heaping tablespoon chopped fresh herb leaves, such as rosemary, sage, tarragon, or oregano, or 1 teaspoon dried herbs**
> **Several fresh parsley sprigs**
> **1 teaspoon black peppercorns, crushed**

Combine all the ingredients. Marinate meats for up to 2 hours at room temperature, or longer in the refrigerator.

YOGURT AND MINT MARINADE *1½ cups*

This Middle Eastern–style marinade is delicious on lamb, beef, and chicken. Skin and deeply score chicken before marinating and oil the cooking rack well.

1¼ cups plain yogurt
3 tablespoons olive oil
2 garlic cloves, minced to a paste
Juice of ¼ lemon
1 teaspoon ground cardamom
2 teaspoons ground fenugreek
1 teaspoon sugar
2 heaping tablespoons chopped fresh mint leaves
Plenty of freshly ground black pepper

Combine all the ingredients and mix well. Marinate meat and poultry at room temperature for up to 2 hours, or longer in the refrigerator.

PORT, ROSEMARY, AND GARLIC MARINADE *1½ cups*

The sweet, full-bodied flavor of port makes a delicious marinade for lamb or beef.

1 cup port
3 tablespoons olive oil
Juice of ½ lemon
1 teaspoon brown sugar
2 tablespoons chopped fresh rosemary leaves,
  or 2 teaspoons dried rosemary
4 to 6 garlic cloves, crushed
Plenty of freshly ground black pepper

Combine all the ingredients. Marinate meats for up to 2 hours at room temperature, or longer in the refrigerator.

BALSAMIC MARINADE *1½ cups*

The slightly sweet, rich flavor of balsamic vinegar flavors this marinade, which is best for beef and lamb.

¼ cup balsamic vinegar
1 cup dry red wine
¼ cup olive oil
2 heaping tablespoons chopped fresh oregano
  leaves, or 2 teaspoons dried oregano
Plenty of freshly ground black pepper

Combine all the ingredients and whisk to emulsify. Marinate meats for up to 2 hours at room temperature, or longer in the refrigerator.

CITRUS MARINADE *1¼ cups*

The combination of citrus juices in this marinade makes it particularly penetrating and gives a tangy taste to food. It goes best with chicken, pork, and shrimp. Make it spicy by adding a slivered chili, such as serrano or jalapeño, and a handful of chopped cilantro.

½ cup freshly squeezed orange juice
¼ cup freshly squeezed lemon juice
2 tablepoons freshly squeezed lime juice
¼ cup olive oil
1 teaspoon honey
2 garlic cloves, sliced into ovals
Plenty of freshly ground black pepper
Several large pieces fresh orange peel

Combine all the ingredients and whisk to emulsify. Marinate meat and poultry for up to 2 hours at room temperature, or 4 hours in the refrigerator. Marinate fish and shellfish for no more than 20 minutes at room temperature or 45 minutes in the refrigerator.

ORANGE AND SOY SAUCE MARINADE *1⅓ cups*

This marinade of Asian flavors is excellent for poultry and flank steak, as well as fish, vegetables, and particularly tofu.

¾ cup freshly squeezed orange juice
¼ cup rice vinegar or cider vinegar
3 tablespoons soy sauce
2 tablespoons peanut oil
2 tablespoons chopped fresh ginger
3 garlic cloves, sliced into ovals
2 green onions, white part and
  half the green, chopped
2 tablespoons chopped fresh cilantro

Combine all the ingredients and whisk to emulsify. Marinate meat, poultry, or tofu for up to 2 hours at room temperature, or longer in the refrigerator. Marinate fish and shellfish for 30 minutes at room temperature, or 1 hour in the refrigerator.

VERMOUTH AND JUNIPER BERRY MARINADE
1½ cups

This intriguing marinade gives food a subtle but sophisticated flavor. It is perfect for beef, pork, or veal.

¼ cup dry vermouth
1 cup dry white wine
¼ cup olive oil
1 tablespoon slightly crushed juniper berries
Several pieces fresh lemon peel
Several fresh parsley sprigs
Plenty of freshly ground black pepper

Combine all the ingredients. Marinate meats for 2 hours at room temperature, or longer in the refrigerator.

BEER AND GRAINY MUSTARD MARINADE
1½ cups

The sweetness of beer in this marinade combines well with pork.

1 bottle medium-bodied beer or ale
2 tablespoons grainy prepared mustard
2 tablespoons vegetable or olive oil
2 teaspoons fennel seed
1 heaping tablespoon chopped fresh sage leaves, or 1 teaspoon dried sage
Plenty of freshly ground black pepper

Combine all the ingredients and whisk to emulsify. Marinate meat or poultry for up to 2 hours at room temperature, or longer in the refrigerator.

MARSALA AND APRICOT MARINADE
2 cups

This marinade is delicious with the delicate flavor of veal, pork, or poultry. Marsala is a fortified Italian wine. Use sweet red Marsala in this recipe.

1½ cups sweet Marsala
¼ cup olive oil
4 dried apricots, sliced into ¼-inch strips
6 fresh thyme sprigs
Plenty of freshly ground black pepper

Combine all the ingredients. Marinate meat or poultry for up to 2 hours at room temperature, or longer in the refrigerator.

TERIYAKI MARINADE
1½ cups

Mirin is a Japanese sweet rice wine used exclusively for cooking. Look for it in the specialty section of the grocery store or in a Japanese market, not a liquor store. The longer food marinates in this delicious sweet marinade, the better. Avoid the hottest fire on the grill for teriyaki, particularly with chicken, since the sugar will burn, but do expect it to caramelize to a dark brown crust. While the food is cooking, simmer the remaining marinade for 15 minutes or so to reduce it, and serve it on the side as a dipping sauce.

⅔ cup soy sauce
½ cup mirin or dry sherry
½ teaspoon Asian sesame oil
2 heaping tablespoons brown sugar
2 large garlic cloves, minced to a paste
2 tablespoons minced fresh ginger

Combine all the ingredients and whisk to emulsify. Marinate meat, poultry, and vegetables for 2 hours at room temperature, or longer in the refrigerator. Marinate fish and shellfish for 30 minutes at room temperature, or 2 hours in the refrigerator.

THAI BARBECUED CHICKEN MARINADE
2 cups

Nam pla is a distinctive fish sauce used in Thai cooking. Palm sugar is a sweetener made either from a type of palm or sugar cane, with a flavor somewhat similar to brown sugar (an acceptable alternative). Find these items in Southeast Asian or Indian markets. Chicken wings or "drumettes" marinated and grilled make excellent appetizers.

1 cup coconut milk
⅓ cup *nam pla*
¼ cup freshly squeezed lime juice
8 garlic cloves, minced
4 shallots, minced
1 cup unsalted roasted peanuts, minced
2 tablespoons curry powder
1 teaspoon dried red pepper flakes
2 tablespoons Thai palm sugar or brown sugar
1 teaspoon salt
½ cup chopped fresh cilantro

Combine all the ingredients and mix well with a wooden spoon. Marinate poultry for 2 hours at room temperature, or 4 hours in the refrigerator.

APPLE-MAPLE MARINADE

1¼ cups

The sweet autumn flavor of maple combines with a hint of apples in this simple marinade. Cook marinated chicken, beef, veal, or pork over a slow fire, taking care not to burn the sugar.

1 cup apple cider, preferably unprocessed
¼ cup maple syrup
1 tablespoon cider vinegar
2 tablespoons vegetable oil
Plenty of freshly ground black pepper
Several pieces fresh lemon peel

Combine all the ingredients. Marinate meat or poultry for up to 2 hours at room temperature, or longer in the refrigerator.

BOURBON AND MUSTARD MARINADE

1½ cups

The bourbon in this marinade gives food a delightful kick.

½ cup bourbon
½ cup dry white wine
¼ cup olive oil
1 heaping tablespoon Dijon-style mustard
¼ cup Worcestershire sauce
2 tablespoons brown sugar
4 green onions, white part only, minced
Plenty of freshly ground black pepper

Combine all the ingredients and whisk to emulsify. Marinate meat or poultry for up to 2 hours at room temperature, or longer in the refrigerator.

CHILI, BASIL, AND SESAME MARINADE

¾ cup

This Thai-style marinade is great for chicken and beef.

½ cup soy sauce
2 tablespoons olive oil
1 tablespoon Asian sesame oil
2 small dried red chili peppers, halved and seeded
1 heaping tablespoon minced fresh ginger
1 tablespoon white sesame seeds, crushed
8 large fresh basil leaves, chopped, or 1 teaspoon dried basil

Combine all the ingredients and whisk to emulsify. Marinate meat or poultry for up to 2 hours at room temperature, or longer in the refrigerator.

TANDOORI MARINADE

2 cups

Garam masala and tamarind paste, which is the fruity, slightly sour flavor in tandoori, are available in Indian markets and sometimes in the specialty section of grocery stores. For tandoori chicken, skin the chicken and score it in several places. It is most important to oil the cooking rack *well* for cooking tandoori.

3 tablespoons coarsely chopped fresh ginger
1 small onion, coarsely chopped
6 garlic cloves
1 heaping tablespoon tamarind paste, seeds removed
⅓ cup olive oil
1¼ cups plain yogurt
2 tablespoons ground cumin
1½ tablespoons *garam masala*
1½ teaspoons turmeric
1 teaspoon paprika
1 teaspoon cayenne
1 teaspoon salt

Combine the ginger, onion, garlic, and tamarind paste in a food processor or blender and process until smooth. Add the remaining ingredients and process again until smooth. Marinate meat and poultry for a minimum of 4 hours in the refrigerator.

LIME AND CHILI MARINADE

1½ cups

This fajita marinade is excellent for strips of beef or pork as well as poultry.

1 cup freshly squeezed lime juice (6 to 8 limes)
¼ cup oil
2 to 3 serrano chilies, seeded and sliced into thick ovals
4 garlic cloves, slightly crushed
2 large onions, thinly sliced
¼ cup chopped fresh cilantro
1 teaspoon cayenne
½ teaspoon salt

Combine all the ingredients. Marinate meat or poultry for 2 hours at room temperature, or longer in the refrigerator.

OIL, BUTTER, PASTE, AND DRY MARINADES

Oil, butter, and *paste* marinades give moistness and flavor to foods. Aromatic oil brushed on the outside seals in juices as food grills, keeping it moist. A butter baste for food before it grills and while it cooks gives it a tasty browning. A paste of dried or fresh herbs, spices, onion, chilies, garlic, citrus peel, ginger, or other flavorings bound with oil creates a flavorful crust that also holds in moisture.

There is no significant amount of an acidic element in oil, butter, or paste marinades, so the penetration of flavors takes place in less than 2 hours at room temperature, and 30 minutes at room temperature for fish. Longer marinades are unnecessary.

Dry marinades season food on the outside, and are usually made up of a combination of herbs and spices. Saltless mixtures can be used instead of salt, since they give the food a highly seasoned flavor. Dry marinades or "sprinkles" need only be added just before grilling, but food sprinkled with a dry mixture will take on a little added flavor if allowed to sit longer.

FLAVOR-INFUSED OILS

To give oil a distinct flavor, add aromatic herbs, spices, garlic, chilies, or citrus peel and let it stand for as little as an hour for just a hint, or up to several weeks for a stronger infusion. Use any oil you like for preparing marinades and bastes for grilling. To a 16-ounce bottle of oil, add one of these suggested ingredients, or try your own combination:

• 3 garlic cloves, slightly crushed, a 1-inch piece of fresh lemon peel, and several black peppercorns
• 2 or more dried red chili peppers
• 2 jalapeño peppers
• A large sprig of fresh rosemary or any fresh herb, and several black peppercorns
• Several large pieces of fresh lemon peel

These oils can be used in paste marinades or salad dressings, or they can be used alone as a light oil baste before grilling food.

BUTTER BASTES

Since butter burns easily, butter bastes are great for quick grilling, when food needs to cook fast and gain a little flavor. Use any of the compound butters on page 50 as a butter baste. Simply melt the flavored butter in a small saucepan and brush on food to be grilled.

For an easier butter baste, melt plain butter over low heat, and add to it spices, herbs, garlic, onion, hot sauce or hot pepper, or any other flavor or combination of flavors. Brush on food for the grill, and baste food occasionally as it grills.

SPICY BUTTER BASTE

Try this on fish and shellfish.

6 tablespoons butter
1 garlic clove, minced to a paste
1 tablespoon dry white wine
Several dashes Louisiana hot sauce or Tabasco sauce
¼ teaspoon cayenne
⅛ teaspoon salt

In a small saucepan, melt the butter over low heat. Whisk in the garlic, white wine, hot sauce, cayenne, and salt.

PASTE MARINADES

Paste marinades are a combination of dry ingredients moistened with just enough oil or other wet ingredient to bind them. The flavorings are ground in a mortar, minced fine, or pulverized in a food processor or coffee grinder, after which oil is added just until the mixture is moist enough to stick to the food.

Some possible ingredients, to be used alone or in combination, include:
• Any fresh or dried herb
• Any dried spice
• Fresh or dried hot chilies
• Grated citrus peel
• Fresh ginger
• Garlic, onions, or shallots

If an ingredient takes on a bitter, charred flavor after grilling, you may want to scrape some of it off before serving. As a general rule, paste marinades are better on foods cooked over a medium-hot or low fire.

PEANUT, GINGER, AND ORANGE PASTE

This paste of Asian flavors is delicious on fish, beef, and chicken. Use boneless, skinless chicken breasts. Oil the cooking rack well, spread the paste on the food sparingly, cook over a medium to low fire, and turn the food carefully to avoid knocking off too much of the crust. When grating the orange, avoid grating the white pith under the peel, since it has a bitter taste. The ingredients can be combined in a food processor or blender for quicker preparation.

½ cup salted roasted peanuts, minced
1 heaping tablespoon minced fresh ginger
2 heaping tablespoons grated fresh orange peel
  (approximately 2 oranges)
2 garlic cloves, minced to a paste
1 heaping tablespoon chopped fresh cilantro
Plenty of freshly ground black pepper
Peanut oil

Mix all the ingredients except the oil together until well blended. Add enough oil so that the dry ingredients are moist and the mixture forms a paste.

GARLIC, PINE NUT, AND TARRAGON PASTE

The earthy flavor of tarragon in this paste goes well with lamb, chicken (boneless, skinless breasts), beef, and fish. Oil the cooking rack well, spread the paste on thinly, and turn the food carefully to avoid knocking off the crust. The ingredients can be combined in a blender or a food processor if desired.

5 garlic cloves, minced to a paste
½ cup pine nuts, minced
2 tablespoons chopped fresh tarragon leaves, or
  2 teaspoons dried tarragon
1 heaping teaspoon grated fresh lemon peel
Plenty of freshly ground black pepper
1 teaspoon freshly squeezed lemon juice
Olive oil

Mix the dry ingredients and the lemon juice together until well blended. Add enough oil so that the dry ingredients are moist and the mixture forms a paste.

MUSTARD PASTE

Tangy mustard complements mild-flavored fish, lamb, veal, beef, and chicken. This paste needs no oil since mustard is the binder. Spread the paste on thinly, cook over a medium to low fire, and turn the food carefully. Be sure to oil the cooking rack well to avoid sticking.

3 tablespoons Dijon-style mustard
1 teaspoon freshly squeezed lemon juice
1 tablespoon brown sugar
1 tablespoon fresh thyme leaves, or 1 teaspoon
  dried thyme
1 tablespoon chopped fresh sage leaves, or
  1 teaspoon dried sage
1 bay leaf, crushed
Plenty of freshly ground black pepper

Mix all the ingredients together until well blended.

SPICY BARBECUE SHAKE

This chili-flavored dry sprinkle is great on almost everything. Brush food with oil or butter before sprinkling on the shake to help it stick, if desired.

2 teaspoons salt
2 tablespoons onion powder
1 teaspoon garlic powder
1 teaspoon chili powder
2 teaspoons dried oregano
2 teaspoons dried thyme
2 teaspoons paprika
1 teaspoon cayenne
1 teaspoon cumin
2 teaspoons dry mustard

Combine all the ingredients.

SALTLESS HERB MIX FOR POULTRY

1 teaspoon dried thyme
1 teaspoon dried sage
½ teaspoon dried oregano
½ teaspoon lavender
2 teaspoons onion powder
½ teaspoon freshly ground black pepper

Combine all the ingredients.

SALTLESS HERB MIX FOR BEEF, LAMB, AND PORK

Brush the meat with oil before sprinkling with this mix to help it stick.

2 teaspoons dried sage
2 teaspoons dried thyme
1 teaspoon dried oregano
3 teaspoons onion powder
1 teaspoon dry mustard
1 teaspoon freshly ground black pepper

Combine all the ingredients.

SALTLESS HERB MIX FOR FISH

Brush the fish with melted butter or oil before sprinkling on the mix.

4 teaspoons dried lemon thyme
2 teaspoons celery seed
1 teaspoon fennel seed, ground
½ teaspoon freshly ground black pepper

Combine all the ingredients.

SAUCES & RELISHES

Sauces and relishes are generally served as flavorful complements to food after it is grilled. They should have an assertive character, to balance the smoky, rich taste of the grilled dish. Some sauces, such as barbecue sauces and compound butters, can be basted on food as it grills, but sauces with sugar or honey burn easily and should only be put on toward the end of cooking or used with a low fire and a covered grill.

YOGURT–CUMIN SAUCE   *¾ cup*

This cool yogurt sauce goes well with spicy grilled chicken and lamb, as well as grilled vegetables of all kinds.

> ½ cup plain yogurt
> 1 tablespoon sour cream
> 1 tablespoon freshly squeezed lemon juice
> 1 green onion, white part and half the green, minced
> 1 small garlic clove, minced to a paste
> 2 teaspoons ground cumin
> Small pinch of sugar
> Salt and freshly ground black pepper to taste

Whisk all the ingredients together until smooth. Serve alongside grilled food.

CAPER VINAIGRETTE   *¾ cup*

The tart, slightly salty flavor of capers goes well with grilled fish.

> ½ cup olive oil
> 2 tablespoons white wine vinegar
> 1 teaspoon Dijon-style mustard
> 1 heaping teaspoon minced fresh tarragon leaves, or ¼ teaspoon dried tarragon
> Small pinch of sugar
> Salt and freshly ground black pepper to taste
> 2 tablespoons capers, drained and slightly crushed

In a small bowl, whisk together the oil, vinegar, tarragon, sugar, and salt and pepper. Add the crushed capers and mix well. Serve over grilled food.

MOLASSES AND BOURBON GLAZE

Brush this on poultry for a rich, mahogany glaze with a sweet flavor.

> 1 tablespoon molasses
> 1 tablespoon bourbon
> 1 tablespoon freshly squeezed orange juice
> 1 teaspoon oil
> ⅛ teaspoon salt
> ¼ teaspoon freshly ground black pepper

Combine the ingredients in a small saucepan over low heat and stir well. Baste food during the last half of grilling.

BOURBON BARBECUE SAUCE   *1½ cups*

This bourbon- and bacon-flavored sauce has a complex range of flavors. Use it as a baste toward the end of cooking and serve it alongside grilled food.

> 3 bacon slices, cooked very crisp, drained, and minced
> 1½ cups ketchup
> ¼ cup molasses
> 2 tablespoons cider vinegar
> 2 tablespoons Worcestershire sauce
> 2 tablespoons bourbon
> 2 tablespoons very strong coffee
> 1 teaspoon dry mustard
> 1 teaspoon onion powder
> 1 scant teaspoon Tabasco sauce

Combine all the ingredients in a non-aluminum saucepan. Bring to a boil, reduce the heat immediately, and simmer over very low heat for 30 minutes, stirring occasionally.

APPLE CREAM SAUCE   *2 cups*

This sweet sauce of lightly cooked apples goes well with grilled meats, particularly pork and ham.

> 2 tablespoons butter
> 2 firm, crisp red apples, not too tart, cored and thinly sliced
> ¼ cup heavy cream
> Salt and freshly ground white pepper to taste
> 1 heaping tablespoon chopped fresh chives

In a skillet, melt the butter over medium heat. Add the apple slices and sauté until just wilted, about 3 minutes, tossing carefully to avoid breaking them.

Add the cream and cook another 1 to 2 minutes. The apple slices should remain intact, and the cream should be mostly cooked off. Season to taste with salt and pepper and add the chives.

Serve alongside grilled food.

ASIAN-STYLE BARBECUE SAUCE

1½ cups

Baste this sweet barbecue sauce on liberally toward the end of cooking. It is delicious on chicken and pork. Hoisin sauce is a sweet Chinese paste made from soybeans, available in the specialty section of most grocery stores.

1 scant cup hoisin sauce
¼ cup soy sauce
3 tablespoons cider vinegar
⅓ cup freshly squeezed orange juice
2 teaspoons dry mustard
2 green onions, white part only, minced

Combine all the ingredients well.

NEW MEXICAN CHILI SAUCE

1¼ cups

New Mexican chilies are the dark red 5- to 7-inch dried chilies you often see gathered in a bunch and hanging in a Southwest-style restaurant or kitchen. They range in flavor from mild to quite hot. This sauce can also be made from milder ancho or pasilla chilies, the dried form of the poblano. Serve this earthy, spicy sauce with grilled chicken and tortillas. Use rubber gloves when handling the chilies.

6 dried New Mexican chilies
½ cup water
2 tablespoons butter
½ red onion, minced
3 garlic cloves, minced
1 tablespoon tomato paste
1 cup chicken broth
½ teaspoon salt

Soak the chilies in hot water to cover for 45 minutes, or until tender. Remove the stems, seeds, and veins, and cut out any dark spots. Puree in a food processor or blender with the water until the mixture is very smooth and the papery skins are chopped fine.

In a large skillet, melt the butter over medium-high heat. Sauté the onion and garlic until translucent, about 5 minutes. Add the pureed chili, tomato paste, chicken broth, and salt. Simmer gently for 30 minutes. Add more water if needed. The sauce should be thick and slightly chunky. It can be pureed again for a smoother sauce.

Serve alongside grilled food.

MUSTARD-MINT SAUCE

1¼ cups

This tangy cold sauce goes well with nearly every kind of grilled food, but particularly lamb, beef, and eggplant.

1 egg yolk
1 tablespoon Dijon-style mustard
1 tablespoon grainy mustard
1 tablespoon white wine vinegar
¼ teaspoon salt
Several grindings black pepper
¾ cup olive oil
1 tablespoon heavy cream
Small pinch of sugar
2 tablespoons chopped fresh mint leaves

Combine the egg yolk, mustards, vinegar, salt, and pepper in a glass or ceramic bowl, or in a blender or food processor. Add the oil, drop by drop, whisking constantly (or with the motor running), until the mixture begins to thicken. Continue adding the remaining oil in a thin stream, whisking constantly. The mixture should be thick and emulsified. Whisk in the cream and sugar and stir in the mint leaves.

Serve alongside grilled food.

COMPOUND BUTTERS

Compound butters are a delicious and simple way to flavor grilled foods. Slice off a pat to melt over just-grilled meats and vegetables, add a dollop to a sauce, or melt a compound butter for basting on food as it grills.

Each of the following combinations requires 1 stick (½ cup) of unsalted butter. Allow the butter to soften in a bowl outside of the refrigerator until it is malleable but not melted. Blend in the flavorings with a wooden spoon. Place the butter in the middle of a sheet of waxed paper or aluminum foil, fold the top half over it, and form the butter into a 6-inch log by rolling the paper into a uniform cylinder. Twist the ends and firm the butter log in the refrigerator. Compound butters can be frozen for several months if tightly wrapped.

Caper: 3 tablespoons crushed drained capers, 1 teaspoon freshly squeezed lemon juice, salt and freshly ground black pepper to taste.

Chive: 2 heaping tablespoons minced fresh chives, salt and freshly ground black pepper to taste.

Garlic: 3 to 4 garlic cloves minced to a paste with a pinch of salt, 1 tablespoon minced fresh parsley, freshly ground white pepper to taste.

Ginger-Garlic: 2 garlic cloves minced to a paste with a pinch of salt, 1 tablespoon minced peeled fresh ginger root, juice of ¼ lemon, several grindings of white pepper.

Hazelnut: ⅓ cup hazelnuts, toasted in a preheated 350° oven for 5 minutes and minced; salt and freshly ground pepper to taste.

Herb: 2 tablespoons minced fresh herb leaves, 1 teaspoon freshly squeezed lemon juice, salt and freshly ground black pepper to taste.

Honey-Mint: 1 tablespoon honey, 1 tablespoon minced fresh mint leaves, salt and freshly ground white pepper to taste.

Honey-Mustard: 1 tablespoon honey, 1 tablespoon Dijon-style or grainy mustard, salt and freshly ground black pepper to taste.

Lemon: Juice of ½ lemon, 1 tablespoon minced fresh lemon peel (the yellow part only, not the white pith), salt and freshly ground white pepper to taste.

Maple: 2 tablespoons maple syrup, salt and freshly ground white pepper to taste.

Olive: 2 tablespoons minced pitted black olives, ½ teaspoon anchovy paste (optional), freshly ground black pepper to taste.

Orange: Juice of ½ orange, 1 tablespoon minced fresh orange peel (the orange part only, not the white pith), salt and freshly ground black pepper to taste.

Pecan: ⅓ cup pecans, toasted in a preheated 350° oven for 5 minutes and minced; salt and freshly ground black pepper to taste.

Pine Nut: ¼ cup pine nuts, toasted until light brown in a preheated 375° oven and minced; salt and freshly ground black pepper to taste.

Toasted Sesame: 1½ tablespoons sesame seeds, toasted in a dry skillet until just beginning to color, and cooled; 2 drops Asian sesame oil, 1 tablespoon minced fresh cilantro, freshly ground black pepper to taste.

CRANBERRY CHUTNEY   *2 cups*

This tart relish is delicious with poultry.

1½ cups fresh cranberries
1 large apple, cored and diced
¼ cup water
1 teaspoon minced fresh ginger
⅓ cup white raisins
3 heaping tablespoons brown sugar

In a medium saucepan, combine the cranberries, apple, water, ginger, and raisins and bring to a boil. Reduce the heat, add the sugar, and simmer uncovered for 7 minutes. Cool to room temperature.

GRILLED RED ONION RELISH   *1½ cups*

Great with steaks or burgers.

1 large red onion, sliced into ⅓-inch-thick slices
1 tablespoon olive oil
1 tablespoon butter
½ teaspoon fennel seed
1 teaspoon fresh thyme leaves,
**   or ½ teaspoon dried thyme**
1 teaspoon red wine vinegar
Salt and freshly ground black pepper to taste

On an open grill over medium-hot coals, cook the red onion slices until tender and browned.

In a skillet over medium-high heat, heat the oil and butter and sauté the grilled red onion slices with the fennel and thyme for 2 to 3 minutes. Add the vinegar and toss the onions another minute. Season to taste with salt and pepper, and serve hot or at room temperature.

PICO DE GALLO   *2½ cups*

This tangy salsa is excellent with grilled fish and chicken, or served with tortilla chips as an appetizer. Serrano chilies are small, deep green chilies of considerable heat. Try jalapeño chilies if serranos are unavailable.

2 large red-ripe tomatoes, chopped
1 medium red onion, chopped
2 to 4 serrano or jalapeño chilies,
**   seeded and minced**
2 garlic cloves, minced
3 heaping tablespoons coarsely
**   chopped fresh cilantro**
2 tablespoons freshly squeezed lime juice
Pinch of sugar
Salt to taste

In a glass or ceramic bowl, combine all the ingredients and mix well. Allow the *pico de gallo* to stand for 1 hour for the flavors to meld. Store for up to 10 days in the refrigerator in a glass jar with a tight-fitting lid.

THREE-PEPPER RELISH *1½ cups*

The sweet flavor of roasted peppers goes well with many grilled dishes, and the combination of colors makes this an attractive relish on the plate.

1 red bell pepper
1 purple bell pepper
1 yellow bell pepper
3 tablespoons olive oil
1 teaspoon balsamic vinegar
1 garlic clove, minced to a paste
Pinch of sugar
2 tablespoons chopped fresh parsley
Salt and freshly ground black pepper to taste

Over a red-hot grill fire, over the open flame of a gas burner, or under a broiler, blister the skins of the peppers all over (they should be quite thoroughly black). Place them in a closed paper bag for 10 minutes to cool and steam. Remove the peppers, core, halve, and seed them, and scrape off all the skin with the blunt side of a knife. Scrape out the ribs on the inside. Do not rinse. Slice the peppers into 1-inch slivers and place them in a bowl.

To the peppers add the oil, vinegar, garlic, sugar, and parsley and toss well to combine. Season to taste with salt and pepper. Serve at room temperature.

TOMATO AND AVOCADO SALSA *4 cups*

Serve alongside spicy meats, or use as an appetizer with tortilla chips.

3 medium red-ripe tomatoes, seeded
  and coarsely chopped
½ red onion, coarsely chopped
1 large ripe avocado, peeled, seeded,
  and very coarsely chopped
3 tablespoons freshly squeezed lime juice
1 tablespoon olive oil
1 large garlic clove, minced to a paste
¼ cup chopped fresh cilantro
Salt and freshly ground black pepper to taste

In a large bowl, combine the tomatoes, onion, and avocado. In a small bowl, whisk the lime juice, oil, and garlic together, pour it over the tomato mixture, and toss gently (your hands are best for this). Add the cilantro, salt and pepper to taste, and toss again.

BASIC MAYONNAISE
1¼ cups

Homemade mayonnaise is a thing unto itself, not resembling at all its grocery store counterpart. It has a fresh, full flavor—slightly eggy with a hint of lemon. Use good-quality oil for mayonnaise, since its flavor will come through. If you like olive oil, by all means use it exclusively, but note that a fruity extra-virgin olive oil makes a better mayo than a lackluster "pure" olive oil. If you like a milder mayonnaise, try safflower or peanut oil, or combine one of those oils with olive oil. The directions here are for mayonnaise made by hand, but the blender or food processor will also serve. Add the oil in a thin stream while the machine is running. One important note: Have *all* the ingredients for mayonnaise at room temperature, and run the bowl under hot water and dry it well before starting.

> **2 egg yolks**
> **1 tablespoon white wine vinegar or freshly**
> ** squeezed lemon juice**
> **½ teaspoon Dijon-style mustard**
> **¼ teaspoon salt**
> **1 to 1¼ cups good-quality oil**
> **2 teaspoons freshly squeezed lemon juice**
> **1 scant tablespoon boiling water**
> **Freshly ground black or white pepper to taste**

In a large bowl, whisk together the yolks, vinegar or lemon juice, mustard, and salt. Begin adding the oil, drop by drop, whisking constantly. When the sauce begins to thicken, add the oil in a thin stream, continuing to whisk vigorously. If the oil gets ahead of you and the mayonnaise starts to separate, stop the flow of oil and whisk for a moment until the sauce coalesces.

When all the oil has been added or the mayonnaise is the desired thickness, whisk in the 2 teaspoons lemon juice. Whisk in the boiling water to set the sauce. Add pepper to taste and more salt if needed. Mayonnaise will keep in the refrigerator for up to 2 weeks.

FLAVORED MAYONNAISES

Use ¾ cup of mayonnaise, preferably homemade (see above) for these delicious flavored mayonnaises. Use yogurt instead of mayonnaise for a sauce lower in fat.

Aïoli: Add 2 to 3 garlic cloves, minced to a paste, to prepared mayonnaise.

Aïoli with Herbs: To aïoli add plenty of minced fresh herb leaves, such as parsley, tarragon, chives, basil, or thyme, or any combination of these.

Avocado: Add 1 well-mashed ripe avocado, 1 teaspoon freshly squeezed lemon juice, and salt and pepper to taste to prepared mayonnaise.

Curry: Add 1 tablespoon curry and the juice of ¼ lemon to prepared mayonnaise and blend well.

Herb: Add plenty of minced fresh herb leaves, such as parsley, tarragon, chives, basil, thyme, or dill, or any combination of these, to prepared mayonnaise.

Mustard: Add 1 heaping tablespoon Dijon-style or grainy mustard, the juice of ½ lemon, and salt and pepper to taste to prepared mayonnaise.

Red Pepper: Add 1 pureed peeled roasted red bell pepper, 1 tablespoon sour cream, and salt and pepper to taste to prepared mayonnaise.

Tomato-Basil: Add ¼ cup pureed tomato and 1 tablespoon minced fresh basil leaves to prepared mayonnaise.

SPICY REMOULADE
1 cup

This mayonnaise-based sauce, spiked with hot pepper sauce and cayenne, is a tangy dipping sauce for grilled seafood, as well as for lightly steamed vegetables served at room temperature.

> **¾ cup mayonnaise, preferably homemade**
> ** (see above)**
> **1 heaping tablespoon Dijon-style mustard**
> **2 green onions, white part and 1 inch of green,**
> ** minced**
> **1 tablespoon chopped cornichons**
> **1 tablespoon crushed drained capers**
> **1 anchovy fillet, minced**
> **1 tablespoon chopped fresh chives**
> **1 tablespoon chopped fresh parsley**
> **¼ teaspoon dried tarragon**
> **½ teaspoon dried chervil**
> **¼ teaspoon cayenne**
> **Several dashes hot pepper sauce**

Combine all the ingredients and mix well. Refrigerate until ready to use.

CHAPTER 4

FROM GRILL TO TABLE

GRILLED ITALIAN APPETIZERS

Smoked Parmigiano with Assorted Breads • Bruschetta with Grilled Eggplant
Scallops Grilled with Basil and Prosciutto • Imported Olives • Grape and Fig Bowl • Dry Italian White Wine

Serves 8 to 10

A wonderful mix of Italian flavors makes up this menu of appetizers for the grill. The tart flavor of hard Italian cheese mellows as it heats, and is delicious on any of the good Italian breads, such as *pane di campagna* (a large, heavy-crusted bread), *pane integrale* (crusty whole-wheat bread), *focaccia,* or saltless bread.

Smoked Parmigiano with Assorted Breads

Use aged Parmigiano-Reggiano or Romano from Italy for the best results.

> **3 slices imported Parmesan or Romano cheese,**
> **⅓ to ½ inch thick (approximately 1½ pounds total)**
> **Olive oil**
> **1 tablespoon chopped fresh herb leaves, such as**
> **rosemary, oregano, marjoram, or thyme**
> **1 jar large grape leaves**
> **Freshly ground black pepper to taste**
> **Assorted breads**

Soak 4 or 5 grapevine cuttings (or a handful of other mild-flavored smoking chips) in water for 30 minutes.

Rub the Parmesan slices well with olive oil and sprinkle one side with herbs. Drain and pat dry 12 to 14 grape leaves and lightly rub them with oil. Arrange them in three stacks at least an inch wider all around than a Parmesan slice.

Put the damp cuttings on medium-hot to low coals and allow them to smoke for a minute or two. Place the leaf stacks on the grill and put a cheese slice in the center of each one. Cover the grill. Melt and smoke the cheese for 3 to 5 minutes.

With a large spatula, lift the grape leaves and cheese slices onto a warm plate and sprinkle with pepper. Serve immediately with assorted breads.

Scallops Grilled with Basil and Prosciutto

If prosciutto is unavailable, Westphalian ham is an excellent substitute.

> **10 to 20 thin slices prosciutto**
> **20 large fresh basil leaves**
> **1½ pounds large sea scallops (approximately 20)**

Soak 10 small wooden skewers in water for 15 minutes.

Cut the prosciutto slices in half crosswise if they are large. Place 1 slice of prosciutto on a flat surface. Place 1 large basil leaf at one end of the slice, and place a large sea scallop on the leaf.

Wrap the prosciutto around the scallop and basil, tucking in the sides, and thread 2 packets onto each skewer.

Grill on an open grill over medium-hot coals until the ham begins to brown and sizzle, 2 to 5 minutes per side.

Bruschetta with Grilled Eggplant

> **1 large eggplant**
> **Salt**
> **1 small red bell pepper**
> **½ cup olive oil**
> **2 garlic cloves, minced to a paste**
> **1 teaspoon balsamic vinegar**
> **¼ cup chopped fresh Italian parsley**
> **Salt and freshly ground black pepper to taste**
> **1 loaf crusty Italian bread**
> **¼ cup capers, drained**

Trim the ends and slice the eggplant into ½-inch-thick slices. Sprinkle the slices lightly with salt and allow to drain on paper towels for 30 minutes. Rinse lightly and pat dry.

Meanwhile, char the red pepper over red-hot coals until blackened all over. Place the pepper in a closed brown paper bag for 10 minutes. Remove and scrape off all the blackened skin with the dull side of a knife. Do not rinse. Stem and seed the pepper and slice it into 1-inch-long slivers.

Brush the eggplant slices lightly with some of the olive oil. Grill the slices over medium-hot coals until browned and tender when pierced with a skewer, approximately 4 minutes per side.

Chop the cooked eggplant and mix in the peppers, garlic, 1 tablespoon of the oil, vinegar, and parsley. Add salt and pepper and set aside until ready to use.

Slice the bread into ⅓-inch-thick slices. Pour the remaining olive oil onto a plate. Grill the bread on both sides until browned. Dip one side quickly in the olive oil. Spread a spoonful of the eggplant mixture on the toasted bread and sprinkle a few capers on top. Serve immediately.

TANDOORI CHICKEN

Papadums • Grilled Tandoori Chicken • Grilled Broccoli with Yogurt-Cumin Sauce
Basmati Rice Pilaf with Mustard and Fennel Seeds • Raita and Chutneys • Lager

Serves 4

The rich, smoky flavor of the *tandoor* oven can be almost perfectly recreated on a grill. The tandoori marinade deeply flavors the chicken, and the high heat of grilling creates a crust on the skinless chicken that keeps it tender and moist. Serve a selection of sweet chutneys along with the *raita*.

Papadums, also called *papads,* are round, very thin crackers made of lentil flour that crisp when heated. Some are made with various flavors mixed in, such as garlic, onion, or pepper. *Papadums* make a great snack at the grill as you are waiting for the coals to reach the cooking stage. Over red-hot coals they will expand and crisp in seconds. When they begin to blister and turn white on the first side, turn them quickly and heat until completely white and just barely beginning to color. Do not let them burn. Find *papadums* in the specialty section of your grocery store with the Indian foods, or in an Indian market.

Grilled Tandoori Chicken

Tandoori paste is available in the specialty section of your grocery store or in Indian markets. You can make the tandoori marinade in this book, or mix ¼ cup prepared tandoori paste with 1½ cups plain yogurt. Try other foods marinated with tandoori paste and grilled, such as white fish fillets or skewered chunks, prawns, scallops, lamb, Cornish game hens, quail, or rabbit.

Special note: Be sure to oil the cooking rack very well before cooking the chicken.

Tandoori Marinade, page 44; see also note above
1 large chicken, cut into 8 pieces

Prepare the Tandoori Marinade. Pull the skin off the chicken pieces and score the flesh with deep diagonal slashes at 1-inch intervals. Toss the chicken well in the marinade, coating all the pieces evenly. Marinate for a minimum of 4 hours in the refrigerator, tossing occasionally to recoat the pieces.

Oil the cooking rack. In a covered grill over medium-hot to low coals, cook the chicken, bone side down, for 15 minutes. Baste the uncooked side with a little of the remaining paste. Turn and grill another 10 to 15 minutes.

Grilled Broccoli with Yogurt-Cumin Sauce

Yogurt-Cumin Sauce, page 48
1½ pounds broccoli

Prepare the Yogurt-Cumin Sauce and refrigerate.

Wash the broccoli and cut into spears, leaving the long stems attached to the florets.

In a covered grill over medium-hot coals, grill the broccoli for approximately 10 minutes, turning several times.

Serve with Yogurt-Cumin Sauce for dipping.

Basmati Rice Pilaf with Mustard and Fennel Seeds

Basmati rice is an aromatic long-grain rice available in the specialty section of your grocery store or in Indian markets.

3 tablespoons olive oil
1½ cups Basmati rice
½ onion, diced
3 cups chicken broth
1 heaping teaspoon mustard seed
1 heaping teaspoon fennel seed
½ teaspoon paprika
¼ teaspoon salt

In a deep saucepan, heat the oil and sauté the rice and onion over medium-high heat until the rice turns opaque and *just* begins to color, about 5 minutes.

Add the chicken broth and bring it to a boil. Add the mustard and fennel seeds, paprika, and salt. Cover with a tight-fitting lid and simmer over low heat for 20 to 25 minutes. The rice should be quite dry. Fluff with a fork and serve.

Raita

This cool, refreshing yogurt dish is a nice foil for the spicy chicken.

¾ cup plain yogurt
1 tablespoon freshly squeezed lemon juice
¼ teaspoon sugar
Salt to taste
1 tablespoon chopped fresh mint leaves
½ cucumber, peeled and diced

Mix all the ingredients together and allow to sit at room temperature for 30 minutes before serving.

RACK OF LAMB WITH PORT, ROSEMARY, AND GARLIC MARINADE

Grilled Rack of Lamb with Port, Rosemary, and Garlic Marinade
Grilled New Potatoes • Sautéed Sugar Snap Peas • Tender Greens Salad

Serves 4

Lamb is perfectly complemented by the flavor of charcoal, and the intense heat seals in the juices and gives the meat a flavorful crust. Try a mix of potato varieties, or use your own favorite. Here we've used Finnish, which taste of sweet butter and have a soft texture.

Grilled Rack of Lamb with Port, Rosemary, and Garlic Marinade

Have the butcher crack the chine between the ribs so they can be cut apart after the rack is cooked.

> **Port, Rosemary, and Garlic Marinade, page 41**
> **One 8-rib rack of lamb, cracked**
> **½ cup heavy cream or half and half**

Prepare the Port, Rosemary, and Garlic Marinade.

Trim some of the fat off the rack, leaving a ⅛-inch layer. Place the rack in a large glass or ceramic dish and pour the marinade over it. Marinate the rack at room temperature for 2 hours, or longer in the refrigerator, turning several times.

Over red-hot coals on an open grill, sear the rack, fat side down, for 1 minute. Turn and sear the other side for 1 minute. Turn the rack again onto the fat side, cover the grill, and cook for approximately 12 minutes. Baste occasionally as the lamb cooks. Turn and cook another 12 minutes, covered, for medium-rare. Test for doneness by carving between the ribs and checking the color. The total cooking time may be 30 minutes or more, depending on the temperature of the fire and the desired doneness.

Remove the rack from the grill. Cover it loosely with a tent of foil. While it rests, pour the marinade into a saucepan and boil it down until reduced by about half. Whisk in the cream and heat through. Carve the lamb into 2-rib portions and serve with the cream sauce.

Grilled New Potatoes

Use metal skewers—they heat up inside the potatoes and speed the cooking. Kosher and coarse sea salt are too coarse for the potatoes, so grind them down somewhat in a mortar or with the back of a wooden spoon.

> **1 dozen new potatoes**
> **Olive oil**
> **Coarse salt**

Scrub the potatoes but do not peel. Rub with olive oil and thread 3 potatoes onto each of 4 metal skewers. Sprinkle with coarse salt. Grill on a covered grill over medium-hot coals, turning often, until brown and tender when pierced with a skewer, 20 to 25 minutes.

Sautéed Sugar Snap Peas

Buy these delicious sweet pods in season. Because they are so tender, they are eaten whole—no shelling is necessary. Break off the little stem, and pull off the tough strings along the sides if the peas are more mature.

> **¾ pound sugar snap peas**
> **3 tablespoons butter**
> **Salt and freshly ground white pepper to taste**

Rinse the pea pods under running water. Pat dry.

Melt the butter in a large skillet over medium-high heat and sauté the pea pods for 3 to 5 minutes. Season with salt and pepper and serve immediately.

Tender Greens Salad

> **1 small head limestone lettuce**
> **½ head butter lettuce**
> **8 fresh basil leaves**
> **¼ cup olive oil**
> **1 tablespoon champagne vinegar**
> **Small pinch of sugar**
> **Salt and freshly ground black pepper**

Gently rinse the lettuces and basil leaves and pat or spin dry. Toss the leaves together.

Combine the olive oil, vinegar, and sugar in the bottom of a salad bowl. Season with salt and pepper. Put the salad greens on top and toss just before serving.

Soft-Shell Crab with Hazelnut Butter

Grilled Soft-Shell Crab with Hazelnut Butter • Grilled Skewered Leeks and Mushrooms
Ribboned Carrot Salad • Fumé Blanc

Serves 6

Every year the Atlantic blue crab sheds its hard outer shell and grows a new one. Just before they shed, the crabs, or "busters," as they are called at this stage, are kept in boxes and plucked out just as they pop their shells. The soft crabs are vulnerable to the hard-shell inmates, and are devoured in a moment if not removed immediately. During this "soft-shell" season, which lasts little more than a week, the crabs can be eaten without shelling, and are perfectly delicious.

Grilled Soft-Shell Crab with Hazelnut Butter

Treat yourself once a year to these delicious crustaceans. They may be expensive, but every bite is pure luxury.

> **Hazelnut Butter, page 50**
> **12 to 18 fresh soft-shell crabs, depending on size**

Prepare the Hazelnut Butter, and mince extra hazelnuts to sprinkle on top of the cooked crabs. Melt the butter gently in a small saucepan and set aside.

To clean the crabs: Pull off the triangular apron on the crab's underside. This kills the crab. Turn it over, lift up the side flaps, and pull off the spongy fingerlike gills that are underneath. Cut off the face just behind the eyes.

Brush the crabs liberally with Hazelnut Butter. Beginning back side down, grill the crabs over medium-hot coals on an open grill for 3 to 5 minutes. Turn and grill another 3 to 5 minutes. Sprinkle extra hazelnuts on the crabs after they are grilled.

Grilled Skewered Leeks and Mushrooms

> **4 medium-sized leeks**
> **24 cultivated mushrooms**
> **Olive oil**
> **Salt**

Soak 12 wood skewers in water for 15 minutes.

Trim the base and green part from the leeks. Rinse very well under running water. Slice into ¾-inch pieces.

Clean the mushrooms well by wiping them with a damp paper towel. Trim off most of the base.

Skewer the leeks and mushrooms horizontally rather than up through the middle. Brush with olive oil and sprinkle with salt. Grill on an open grill over medium-hot coals, turning frequently, for 10 to 12 minutes, or until the leeks and mushrooms begin to brown.

Ribboned Carrot Salad

This carrot salad is simple and refreshing. Look for carrots free of cracks and dryness.

> **1½ pounds carrots**
> **2 tablespoons freshly squeezed lemon juice**
> **1 tablespoon freshly squeezed orange juice**
> **2 teaspoons olive oil**
> **½ teaspoon rosewater (optional)**
> **1 tablespoon sugar**
> **⅛ teaspoon salt**
> **Freshly ground white pepper to taste**
> **1 green onion, white part and half the green, coarsely chopped**

Peel the carrots with a sharp vegetable peeler and discard the outer peels. With the peeler, square off the carrot, taking off long strips about ⅜-inch wide. Work your way around each carrot peeling off the sides evenly until the carrot becomes difficult to peel. Put the strips in a large bowl.

In a small bowl, whisk together the lemon juice, orange juice, olive oil, rosewater, sugar, salt, and several grindings of pepper. Pour over the carrots and toss gently to coat them. Cover with plastic wrap and refrigerate for 1 hour.

Lift the carrots out of the liquid in the bowl and place in a serving dish. Sprinkle with chopped green onion.

BURGERS AND RED ONION SLICES

Grilled Burgers and Red Onion Slices • Salad of Grilled Potato and Fennel
Sliced Beefsteak Tomatoes • Poppyseed Kaiser Rolls • Red Wine

Serves 6

The charbroiled hamburger is just plain good eating. It is most definitely pure American cuisine, and we nearly all have deep convictions about what constitutes "the perfect burger." For the purist, burgers can only be made from ground beef chuck or sirloin. But ground turkey also makes a delicious burger, especially if the meat is first mixed with a beaten egg, chopped garlic, and fresh herbs.

Grilled Burgers and Red Onion Slices

For a "classic" hamburger, use freshly ground beef chuck with a fat content of about 20 percent. This may sound high, but it makes a juicier, more flavorful burger, and on the grill a lot of the fat will render out. For a "steakier," firmer, less juicy hamburger, use ground sirloin. In either case, do not over-compress the meat when you make the patties, as this breaks down the fat and makes the burger dry.

**3 pounds ground beef chuck or sirloin
  (about 20 percent fat)
2 tablespoons chopped fresh sage leaves,
  or 2 teaspoons dried sage
2 garlic cloves, minced
1½ teaspoons salt
Plenty of freshly ground pepper
2 large red onions
Olive oil
6 poppyseed Kaiser rolls**

In a large bowl, place the ground beef, sage, garlic, salt, and pepper. Toss the ingredients gently with your fingers, mixing as little as possible. Form the beef into six or eight ¾-inch-thick patties. Avoid overpacking the patties.

Peel the red onions and slice into ½-inch-thick rounds. Rub the slices with olive oil.

On on open grill over red-hot to medium-hot coals, cook the burgers for approximately 4 minutes on the first side, then 4 minutes on the second side for rare, 4 to 5 minutes for medium-rare, 6 minutes for medium, and 7 for well done. Grill the onion slices until browned and tender, approximately 4 minutes per side. Cover the grill momentarily to extinguish flare-ups if necessary.

Serve the burgers with poppyseed Kaiser rolls.

Salad of Grilled Potatoes and Fennel

This salad can be prepared a bit in advance and served at room temperature.

**¾ cup mayonnaise, preferably homemade
  (see page 53)
2 tablespoons heavy cream or half and half
1 small garlic clove, minced to a paste
2 green onions, white part and half the green,
  minced
2 teaspoons sugar
Salt and freshly ground black pepper to taste
1 large fresh fennel bulb, or 2 small bulbs
4 medium-sized boiling or red potatoes,
  scrubbed but not peeled
Olive oil**

Prepare the mayonnaise. Into the mayonnaise whisk the cream or half and half, garlic, green onions, and sugar until smooth. Season with salt and pepper and refrigerate until ready to use.

Slice the white bulb of the fennel vertically into ¼-inch-thick slices, securing the layers with skewers. Reserve several sprigs of fennel leaves for garnish. Slice the potatoes into ¼-inch-thick slices. Brush the fennel and potato slices with olive oil. Grill the potatoes in a covered grill over medium-hot coals until browned and tender when pierced with a skewer, 3 to 5 minutes per side. Grill the fennel slices for 2 minutes per side. Allow both to cool. Slice the fennel into sticks.

Arrange the cooked potato slices on a platter and pile the fennel sticks in the center. Drizzle with the mayonnaise dressing, and sprinkle the fennel leaves on top.

Sliced Beefsteak Tomatoes

**1 bunch watercress
3 ripe large beefsteak tomatoes,
  or other ripe large tomatoes
Olive oil
Several fresh parsley sprigs, chopped
Freshly ground black pepper to taste**

Wash the watercress in a sink of cold water and drain. Trim off the bottom half of the stems. Arrange the watercress on a large plate.

Rinse the tomatoes and pat dry. Remove the stems. Slice into ½-inch-thick slices and arrange on top of the watercress.

Drizzle the tomatoes with olive oil and sprinkle liberally with chopped parsley and pepper.

BONELESS QUAIL WITH CORN BREAD AND ESCAROLE STUFFING

Grilled Boneless Quail with Corn Bread and Escarole Stuffing
Grilled Parsnips • Steamed Asparagus • White Wine

Serves 4

The Molasses and Bourbon Glaze enhances the delightful, sweet flavor of quail on the grill. The savory corn bread stuffing fills out the tiny quails, which makes them easy to serve and to eat. Boneless quail, with the body cavity boned out and the leg bones still intact, are difficult to find but well worth the effort. Look for a game distributor in your town or a mail order outfit that will ship them frozen.

Grilled Boneless Quail with Corn Bread and Escarole Stuffing

One quail is usually about 3½ ounces, so allow 2 quails per person, unless you are using bobwhites. They are slightly larger, and 1 to 1½ will serve 1 person.

> 1 head escarole
> 5 bacon slices, chopped
> 3 shallots, minced
> ¼ cup pine nuts
> 2 garlic cloves, minced
> 2 teaspoons fresh thyme leaves,
>   or ½ teaspoon dried thyme
> 2 cups crumbled dried corn bread
> ⅓ cup chicken broth
> Molasses and Bourbon Glaze, page 48
> 8 boneless quail

Separate the leaves of the escarole and rinse them under running water to remove the grit. Break off part of the white rib. Do not dry the leaves.

In a large skillet, slowly sauté the bacon pieces until they are lightly browned. Remove them with a slotted spoon to paper towels. Pour off all but 1 tablespoon of the fat.

Add the shallots and pine nuts to the bacon fat and sauté for 3 minutes. Add the garlic and sauté the mixture another minute. Add the escarole leaves, turn the heat to high, cover, and cook until the leaves are wilted, about 2 minutes. Remove the mixture to a cutting board and chop it fine.

Return the escarole to the skillet; add the thyme, bread crumbs, and bacon. Pour the broth over the mixture and toss it over medium heat for a minute or so. Set aside to cool slightly.

Prepare the Molasses and Bourbon Glaze.

Stuff each quail with about 3 tablespoons of corn bread stuffing, manipulating the stuffing so that it "reshapes" the boneless bird. Brush the quail with the glaze.

In a covered grill over medium-hot to slow coals, cook the birds first breast-side down for 6 to 8 minutes, then turn and cook an additional 6 to 8 minutes, depending on the size of the quail. Brush once with the glaze during grilling. The birds are done when the legs point sharply up and the juices run clear when pierced with a skewer. The meat of quail is naturally red, even when cooked.

Grilled Parsnips

This root vegetable looks like a white carrot and is absolutely delicious grilled.

> 4 medium-sized to small parsnips
> Olive oil
> Salt to taste

Scrub the parsnips, but do not peel. Trim the ends if desired and slice lengthwise into ¼-inch-thick slices. Rub with olive oil and sprinkle lightly with salt.

Grill the parsnip slices in a covered grill over medium-hot coals for 5 minutes per side, or until lightly browned and tender when pierced with a skewer.

Steamed Asparagus

> 1½ pounds thin asparagus
> Butter and salt to taste (optional)

Rinse the asparagus and bend each stalk carefully until it breaks at its natural breaking point (this removes the tough end). Steam for 5 minutes, or until just tender and bright green but still crunchy. Serve as is or with a little butter and salt.

PEPPERS STUFFED WITH EGGPLANT

Grilled Peppers Stuffed with Eggplant • Grilled Skewered Summer Squash with Rosemary Oil
Sliced Fruit with Yogurt-Mint Dressing • White Wine

Serves 4

Grilling is traditionally linked with the cooking of meats; seldom do we think of a grilled vegetarian meal. But charcoal brings out terrific flavors in vegetables, and many combinations can be made to create a non-meat meal.

Grilled Peppers Stuffed with Eggplant

Select large, firm red or yellow bell peppers, free of mushy spots or cracks. The luxurious Holland bell peppers are particularly delicious. The pepper skins become charred on the grill—either peel the blackened skin off the whole pepper as you eat it or scrape the sweet flesh from the skin.

1 medium-sized eggplant
Salt
¼ cup olive oil
1 cup bread crumbs
2 garlic cloves, minced to a paste with
**   a pinch of salt**
½ cup freshly grated Parmesan cheese
¼ cup pine nuts
¼ cup chopped fresh Italian parsley
1 tablespoon chopped fresh herb leaves,
**   such as basil, marjoram, thyme, or oregano**
1 egg, beaten
6 red or yellow bell peppers

Slice the eggplant into ¼-inch-thick slices. Salt lightly and set aside on paper towels to drain for one-half hour. Rinse lightly and pat dry. Chop coarsely. In a large skillet, heat the oil and sauté the eggplant over high heat until browned and tender, approximately 5 minutes.

Chop the cooked eggplant again and combine it with the bread crumbs, garlic, Parmesan, pine nuts, parsley, and herbs in a bowl. Add the beaten egg and mix well. Cut the tops off the peppers and remove and discard the seeds and whitish core from both the tops and from inside the peppers. Reserve the tops.

Stuff the eggplant mixture loosely into the peppers. Secure the tops to the peppers with toothpicks. Cook the peppers in a covered grill over a medium-hot to low fire for 1 hour, turning occasionally.

Grilled Skewered Summer Squash with Rosemary Oil

Cook the squash on the grill before cooking the peppers and serve them at room temperature. You can also use skewered whole baby squash for this dish.

Rosemary Oil, page 45
6 assorted summer squashes, such as crookneck,
**   summer, zucchini, or pattypan**
Salt

Prepare the Rosemary Oil and set aside.

Soak 6 wood skewers in water for 15 minutes.

Cut the squash into 1-inch pieces. Skewer the squash pieces, alternating the varieties. Brush with the flavored oil and sprinkle with salt. Grill on an open or covered grill over a medium-hot fire for about 10 minutes, turning occasionally.

Sliced Fruit with Yogurt-Mint Dressing

Pick out an assortment of the freshest fruit in season.

Assorted fruit, peeled if desired and sliced

Yogurt-Mint Dressing
½ cup plain yogurt
1 tablespoon freshly squeezed lemon juice
1 tablespoon brown sugar
2 tablespoons chopped fresh mint leaves

Arrange sliced and whole fruit on a serving dish.

Whisk the yogurt, lemon juice, brown sugar, and mint together and drizzle it over the fruit.

PRAWNS WITH SPICY REMOULADE

Grilled Prawns with Spicy Remoulade • Steamed Greens
Grilled Cornmeal Mush Slices • Chardonnay

Serves 4

Little patches of Louisiana and Southern cooking are sewn into this menu of spicy prawns and tangy greens served up with cornmeal mush (our version is buttered and grilled rather than fried). A nice Louisiana-style alternative would be to grill crayfish, or crawdads, along with the prawns. Buy live crayfish, rinse them in several changes of water, and discard any that do not move. Plunge them into boiling water, cook for 4 minutes, and let cool. Brush the crayfish with Spicy Butter Baste 30 minutes before grilling. Grill the crayfish over hot coals, turning them several times, for 6 to 8 minutes. Peel off the tail shell and eat!

Grilled Prawns with Spicy Remoulade

Prawns and jumbo shrimp are delicious grilled with this Spicy Butter Baste. Select large fresh shrimp or prawns with a nice, clean smell.

> **Spicy Remoulade, page 53**
> **12 to 20 fresh prawns, depending on size**
> **Spicy Butter Baste, page 45**

Prepare the Spicy Remoulade and refrigerate until ready to use.

Peel the shell from all but the last section and tail fin of the prawns and rinse under cool running water. Pat dry. Soak 6 to 8 wood skewers in water for 15 minutes.

Prepare the Spicy Butter Baste. Thread 3 prawns onto each skewer (depending on size) and brush them liberally with the baste. Set aside for 30 minutes.

Grill the skewered prawns on an open grill over red-hot to medium-hot coals for approximately 3 minutes per side, basting twice while they cook. Prawns are done when just pink and opaque. Serve immediately, with Spicy Remoulade on the side for dipping.

Steamed Greens

Use collards, kale, mustard, beet, or turnip greens for this recipe. You can also use them in combination, or mixed with spinach or Swiss chard for a milder dish.

> **2 pounds greens**
> **2 shallots, coarsely chopped**
> **1 tablespoon cider vinegar**
> **Salt and freshly ground black pepper to taste**

Wash the greens very thoroughly in several changes of cold water. Cut off the stems and any tough ribs on the backs of the leaves. Slice the leaves crosswise into 1-inch-wide strips.

Place the greens and chopped shallots in a steamer basket and steam over boiling water in a large, covered pot for about 15 minutes or until tender. Remove them to a bowl and toss the hot greens with the vinegar. Season to taste and serve immediately.

Grilled Cornmeal Mush Slices

Prepare the mush well in advance to allow it to firm completely. Try dipping the grilled slices into the Spicy Remoulade along with the prawns.

> **1 cup cornmeal**
> **3 cups water**
> **1 teaspoon salt**
> **1 cup fresh or defrosted frozen corn kernels**
> **¼ red bell pepper, minced**
> **2 tablespoons sour cream**
> **Several dashes Worcestershire sauce**
> **Several dashes Tabasco sauce**
> **Salt and freshly ground black pepper to taste**
> **Spicy Butter Baste, page 45**

In a medium bowl, mix the cornmeal with 1 cup of the water. In a large saucepan, bring the remaining 2 cups of water and the salt to a boil. Add the cornmeal mixture to the boiling water and cook, stirring often, over low heat for 6 minutes, or until thick.

Stir in the corn kernels, red pepper, sour cream, Worcestershire sauce, and Tabasco, and cook another minute or so. Adjust the seasonings. Spread the mixture into a buttered loaf pan. Cool to room temperature and then place in the refrigerator overnight, or until quite firm.

Prepare the Spicy Butter Baste (if you are preparing the prawns, above, one recipe of the baste is ample for both dishes).

Cut the cooled cornmeal mixture into ½-inch-thick slices. Brush with baste and grill on an open grill over red-hot to medium-hot coals until browned and heated through, approximately 5 minutes per side.

TENDERLOIN OF BEEF WITH MUSTARD-MINT SAUCE

Grilled Tenderloin of Beef with Mustard-Mint Sauce • Couscous with Sautéed Figs
Steamed Artichokes with Creamy Vinaigrette • Pinot Noir

Serves 8

Beef tenderloin, also called beef filet, is the most tender cut of beef and thus the most expensive. It cooks beautifully on the grill over hot coals, giving the meat a slightly charred exterior while the inside remains juicy and tender. Serve it with tangy Mustard-Mint Sauce and couscous to soak up the delicious juices.

Grilled Tenderloin of Beef with Mustard-Mint Sauce

Have the butcher trim off any connective tissue and excess fat. The tenderloin tapers at one end, which gives you a nice range of doneness.

Mustard-Mint Sauce, page 49
1 whole beef tenderloin (4½ to 5 pounds)
Olive oil
Freshly ground black pepper

Prepare the Mustard-Mint Sauce and set aside.

Bring the tenderloin to room temperature before grilling. If the "tail" end is very thin, fold it under and secure it with a toothpick. Brush the beef liberally with the oil and sprinkle with pepper. Oil the cooking rack. On an open grill over red-hot coals, sear the tenderloin on 2 sides for 1½ to 2 minutes each. Cover the grill and partially close the vents, and cook the tenderloin for approximately 10 minutes per side for rare, or until a meat thermometer registers 120°. Cook the meat for 3 to 4 minutes longer for more doneness, or until the thermometer registers 130° for rare to medium-rare, 140° for medium, and 155° for well done.

Remove the tenderloin from the grill and cover it loosely with aluminum foil for 5 minutes before carving to allow the juices to set.

Slice the meat into ¾-inch-thick medallions and serve with several spoonfuls of sauce.

Couscous with Sautéed Figs

Couscous is a North African "pasta" made from medium-grain semolina. It is somewhat time-consuming to prepare from the uncooked grain, so we recommend the precooked or quick-cooking variety, available in the rice and grain section of most markets.

1½ cups chicken broth
1½ cups water
2 tablespoons olive oil
Pinch of salt
2 cups quick-cooking couscous
4 dried figs, slivered
2 tablespoons butter
2 tablespoons chopped fresh Italian parsley

Bring the broth, water, oil, and salt to a boil in a large saucepan. Stir in the couscous, cover, and remove the pan from the heat. Let stand 7 minutes.

Meanwhile, sauté the figs in butter over low heat until tender, about 3 minutes. Fluff the couscous with a fork and toss in the figs and parsley.

Steamed Artichokes with Creamy Vinaigrette

4 large artichokes
1 lemon, cut in half
1 teaspoon peppercorns
1 bay leaf
1 teaspoon olive oil

Creamy Vinaigrette
¼ cup white wine vinegar
1 tablespoon Dijon-style mustard
Pinch of sugar
1 to 1¼ cups olive oil
⅓ cup heavy cream
Salt and freshly ground black pepper to taste

Rinse the artichokes well under running water. Allow the water to run down into the leaves, then shake it out, repeating this several times. With kitchen shears, trim off the spiky tips of the leaves. Trim the bases to ½ inch. Rub the outsides of the artichokes all over with a cut half of the lemon.

Into a large pot, pour water to a depth of 1 inch and add the lemon halves, peppercorns, bay leaf, and oil. Place the artichokes in a steamer basket and set it in the pot, or arrange them base down in the pot. Bring the water to a boil, cover, and steam the artichokes over medium heat for 30 to 45 minutes, depending on size, or until a leaf pulls off easily and the flesh on the inside of the leaf is tender (you will need to check the water level every 10 minutes or so and add more water if needed). Run the artichokes briefly under cold water and drain them upside down until cool.

While the artichokes are cooling, prepare the Creamy Vinaigrette: In a medium bowl, combine the vinegar, mustard, and sugar. Whisk in the oil until emulsified. Whisk in the cream and adjust the seasoning. Halve the artichokes and gently scrape out the chokes. Serve the artichokes at room temperature, drizzled with the vinaigrette.

CALVES' LIVER WITH SAGE BUTTER AND PANCETTA

Grilled Calves' Liver with Sage Butter and Pancetta • Tuscan White Beans with Grilled Red Onion
Romaine Lettuce Salad with Creamy Parmesan Dressing • Saltless Italian Bread • Pinot Noir

Serves 6

This Italian twist on liver and bacon goes beyond the ordinary. Liver is delicious grilled quickly over a hot fire with a dollop of sage-flavored butter melted over it, transforming a humble dish into a sophisticated combination of flavors.

Grilled Calves' Liver with Sage Butter and Pancetta

Pancetta is Italian bacon that generally comes in a large roll rather than as a slab. Have the butcher slice thin rounds for this recipe.

Sage Butter, see Herb Butter, page 50
1½ pounds calves' liver, membrane removed, sliced ½ inch thick and cut into serving-sized pieces
6 slices pancetta

Prepare the Sage Butter. Melt 3 tablespoons in a small saucepan. Brush the liver slices generously with the melted butter.

On an open grill over red-hot coals, grill the liver for 2 to 3 minutes per side, basting it occasionally with the remaining butter. Grill the pancetta over red-hot coals for 2 to 3 minutes per side.

Put a piece of pancetta on each plate and a dollop of Sage Butter on each serving of liver.

Tuscan White Beans with Grilled Red Onion

2 cups dried white beans
6 cups water
½ teaspoon salt
1 bay leaf, 1 thyme sprig, 1 sage sprig
⅓ cup extra-virgin olive oil
2 tablespoons balsamic vinegar
1 teaspoon Dijon-style mustard
2 garlic cloves, minced to a paste with a pinch of salt
Small pinch of sugar
Salt and freshly ground black pepper to taste
1 large red onion, cut into ½-inch-thick rounds
8 large fresh basil leaves, sliced into thin ribbons
6 fresh sage leaves, chopped
¼ cup chopped fresh Italian parsley

Pick through the beans and remove any rocks. Soak the beans overnight in plenty of water, or, for quick soaking, bring the beans to a boil in a large pot with plenty of water, boil 1 minute, cover, and let stand for 1 hour.

Drain the beans. In a large pot, bring the 6 cups of water to a boil with the salt. Add the beans, bay leaf, and thyme and sage sprigs and return to a boil. Reduce the heat and simmer, covered, until the beans are tender but still hold their shape, 30 to 45 minutes.

In a small bowl, whisk together the oil, vinegar, mustard, garlic, and sugar. Drain the cooked beans, put them in a bowl, and pour the oil-vinegar mixture over the hot beans. Toss well to combine. Season to taste with salt and pepper.

Grill the onion slices on an open grill over medium-hot coals for 5 minutes per side. They should be tender and browning. Slit the rings on one side so they uncurl into long strips. Toss the grilled onion slices, basil, sage, and parsley with the beans. Serve slightly warm or at room temperature.

Romaine Lettuce Salad with Creamy Parmesan Dressing

If romaine lettuce is unavailable, try tender red leaf lettuce, as shown here.

3 small heads romaine lettuce

Creamy Parmesan Dressing
1 egg yolk
2 teaspoons white wine vinegar
2 teaspoons minced shallot
1 garlic clove, minced to a paste
¼ teaspoon salt
½ cup olive oil
2 tablespoons heavy cream or half and half
Generous ⅓ cup grated Parmesan cheese
Freshly ground black pepper to taste

Pull the coarse leaves off the heads of romaine, leaving the tender inner leaves attached to the base. Slice each head lengthwise and rinse well. Drain. Slice off 1 inch of the base, but do not separate the leaves. Cover with a damp paper towel and place in the refrigerator until needed.

In a warmed glass or ceramic bowl, whisk together the egg yolk, vinegar, shallot, garlic, and salt until well blended. Add the oil in a slow, steady stream, whisking constantly. When all the oil has been added and the sauce is thick, whisk in the cream and Parmesan. Season with several grindings of pepper. Drizzle the dressing over each romaine half and serve.

LIME-MARINATED ROCK CORNISH GAME HENS

Grilled Lime-marinated Rock Cornish Game Hens • Baked Black Beans, Corn, and Green Chilies
Mixed Green Salad with Orange Vinaigrette • Warm Tortillas • Beer

Serves 6

The distinctive fajita-style marinade in this menu is made of tart lime, cilantro, and onion, flavors that combine well with the smoke of the grill. Serve these hens with tortillas heated lightly on the grill, a wedge of lime, and plenty of salsa, chopped onion, cilantro, and sliced avocado for making individual combinations.

Grilled Lime-marinated Rock Cornish Game Hens

One small Rock Cornish game hen is an ample serving for a hearty eater; larger ones can be split for two servings.

Lime and Chili Marinade, page 44
3 to 6 Rock Cornish game hens, depending on size

Prepare the Lime and Chili Marinade and set aside.

Rinse the hens and pat dry. Flatten the hens for grilling by first cutting down one side of the backbone from tail to neck, then cutting down the other side of the backbone to remove and discard it. Place each hen breast-side up on a flat surface and press sharply with the heel of your hand on the breastbone to flatten the bird completely. Tuck the wings under the breasts. With a small sharp knife, make a small slit through the apron of skin between the breast and thigh, repeat this on the other side of the hen, and tuck each leg down through the slits. Trim off the excess fat. Place the flattened hens bone-side down in a large glass or ceramic dish and pour the marinade over them. Marinate at room temperature for 2 hours, or longer in the refrigerator. Remove from the refrigerator 30 minutes before grilling.

Oil the cooking rack. On an open grill over red-hot to medium-hot coals, sear skin-side down for 1½ minutes. Turn and sear the other side for 1 minute. Leave the hens bone-side down, cover the grill, and cook them 10 minutes on the first side, and 8 to 10 minutes on the second side. Baste the hens several times with the marinade while they are cooking.

Baked Black Beans, Corn, and Green Chilies

This delicious dish can be assembled in advance and heated just before serving.

1½ cups dried black beans
1 bay leaf
1 teaspoon salt
3 tablespoons olive oil
1 large red onion, thinly sliced

1 mild green chili, such as Anaheim or poblano, seeded, cored, and sliced into slivers
3 large garlic cloves, minced to a paste
2 cups fresh, defrosted frozen, or drained canned corn kernels
½ bunch fresh cilantro, chopped
Salt and freshly ground pepper to taste
1 cup grated sharp Cheddar cheese
½ cup sour cream

Wash and pick over the beans. Soak the beans overnight in plenty of water, or, for quick soaking, bring them to a boil with water to cover in a large pot, remove from heat, and let stand, covered, for 1 hour.

Drain the beans. Put them back in the pot, cover with plenty of water, and add the bay leaf and salt. Bring to a boil, then reduce the heat and simmer, uncovered, until the beans are tender but still hold their shape, approximately 45 minutes. Drain the beans.

Meanwhile, preheat the oven to 375°. Heat the oil in a large skillet. Sauté the onion slices over medium heat for about 10 minutes. Add the green chili and garlic and sauté another 2 minutes.

Add the onion mixture to the beans along with the corn kernels and ¼ cup of the chopped cilantro. Season to taste with salt and pepper. Put the beans in a casserole and sprinkle with the grated cheese. Heat for 20 minutes, or until the cheese is melted and bubbly on top. Serve with dollops of sour cream and sprinkle with the remaining chopped cilantro.

Mixed Green Salad with Orange Vinaigrette

1 small head butter or limestone lettuce
1 small head red leaf lettuce
½ small head curly endive

Orange Vinaigrette

6 tablespoons walnut oil
2 tablespoons freshly squeezed orange juice
2 teaspoons white wine vinegar
1 green onion, minced
Small pinch of sugar
Salt and freshly ground black pepper to taste
1 tablespoon very finely slivered fresh orange peel

Wash the lettuces and endive thoroughly and dry well. Tear into large pieces. In a glass or ceramic bowl, combine the oil, orange juice, vinegar, green onion, sugar, and salt and pepper. Whisk to emulsify. Adjust the seasonings. Toss the lettuce and endive with the vinaigrette, sprinkle with orange peel, and serve.

HAM STEAK WITH APPLE CREAM SAUCE

Grilled Ham Steak with Apple Cream Sauce • Grilled Sweet Potatoes
Braised Escarole • Popovers • Rosé

Serves 4

Slightly salty, rich ham combines well with the smoky flavor of the grill, and is balanced by the sweet Apple Cream Sauce and grilled sweet potatoes.

Grilled Ham Steak with Apple Cream Sauce

Look for ham with the bone in.

> **4 tablespoons butter, melted**
> **1 tablespoon fresh thyme leaves,**
> **or 1 teaspoon dried thyme**
> **Several grindings black pepper**
> **2 fresh ham steaks, ¾ to 1 pound each**
> **and ½ inch thick**
> **Apple Cream Sauce, page 48**

To the melted butter, add the thyme and black pepper. Brush the ham steaks with the butter. On an open grill over red-hot coals, sear the steaks for 1 minute per side. Cover the grill and continue to cook the steaks for 5 minutes per side, basting with the remaining butter.

While the steaks are cooking, prepare the Apple Cream Sauce. Serve the cooked ham steaks with the sauce on top.

Grilled Sweet Potatoes

Sweet potatoes cooked on the grill are a simple treat.

> **3 medium-sized sweet potatoes**
> **Olive oil**

Scrub the sweet potatoes and rinse well but do not peel. Slice them into ¼-inch-thick slices. Rub the slices with olive oil. Cook the sweet potatoes in a covered grill over medium-hot coals for approximately 5 minutes per side, or until they are browned and tender when pierced with a skewer.

Braised Escarole

You can substitute curly endive (also called *frisée*) in this recipe.

> **1 head escarole**
> **3 tablespoons olive oil**
> **3 tablespoons chicken broth**
> **Salt and pepper to taste**
> **1 lemon, quartered**

Slice the escarole lengthwise into quarters. Rinse each quarter under running water, allowing the water to run between the leaves but taking care not to break the leaves off the base. Drain well.

In a large skillet, heat the olive oil over medium-high heat. Place the escarole quarters cut-side down in the skillet and brown briefly. Add the chicken broth (or water), cover, and cook 3 to 5 minutes. The liquid will be mostly absorbed, and the stems of the escarole will be tender when pierced with a skewer.

Serve the escarole quarters cut side up, season with salt and pepper, and serve with the lemon wedges.

Popovers

Resist opening the oven while these custardy muffins cook and they'll be perfect every time. This recipe makes 8 popovers.

> **1 cup unbleached all-purpose flour**
> **½ teaspoon salt**
> **2 eggs**
> **1 cup milk**
> **2 tablespoons butter**

Preheat the oven to 425°. Place the popover pan in the oven while it is preheating so that the pan will get very hot.

Measure the flour and salt into a mixing bowl. In another bowl, beat the eggs and milk together, pour them into the flour, and combine well with a rotary beater or whisk until smooth.

Remove the hot popover pan from the oven and put a small piece of butter in each cup. Fill each cup a little over half full and bake for 35 minutes without opening the oven. Serve hot with plenty of butter.

GRAPEVINE-SMOKED SALMON, TROUT, AND OYSTERS

Grapevine-smoked Salmon, Trout, and Oysters • Fresh and Dried Bean Salad
Oven-roasted Asparagus • Assorted Breads and Herbed Cream Cheese • White Wine

Serves 8 to 10

Though smoking requires time, it does not require vigilance, and this menu comes together with unexpected ease. All the elements of this buffet dinner or elegant picnic are most flavorful served at room temperature.

Grapevine-smoked Salmon, Trout, and Oysters

Sablefish, steelhead, whitefish, and butterfish are also delicious prepared this way, as are mussels and clams.

1 fillet of fresh salmon, skin on
(approximately 2½ pounds)
2 pan-dressed trout (1½ to 2 pounds each)
Olive oil
2 dozen oysters
½ bottle dry white wine
4 cups water
Several large pieces fresh lemon peel
Several fresh dill sprigs

Place a handful of grapevine chunks or dried grapevines in water to cover and soak for 1 hour.

Rub the salmon and trout liberally with oil, and scrub the oysters with a stiff brush.

Prepare a charcoal-water smoker according to the instructions on page 31, or use a grill or gas grill as a smoker (see Chapter 3, "On Smoking"). Heat the wine and water in a saucepan. Into the water pan of the smoker carefully pour the heated wine and water, and add the lemon peel and dill sprigs to the liquid. Oil both the bottom and top cooking racks. Put the salmon, skin-side down, and the trout on the bottom rack, and arrange the oysters in one layer on the top rack.

Add several grapevine chunks to the fire. Smoke-cook the oysters for 1 to 1½ hours, or until the meat is firm. Discard any that do not open. Continue smoking the salmon and trout for another 1 to 1½ hours, or until they flake with a fork. Add more grapevine chunks, charcoal, and water to the water pan as needed.

Fresh and Dried Bean Salad with Chive Vinaigrette

Use any combination of dried beans, including black-eyed peas, flageolets, kidney beans, limas, pink beans, pintos, black beans, and so on. Select fresh beans in season.

1 cup dried pinto beans
1 cup dried red flageolets
1 cup dried small white beans
3 teaspoons salt

Chive Vinaigrette
1½ cups olive oil
⅓ cup red wine vinegar
2 tablespoons Dijon-style mustard
4 garlic cloves, minced to a paste
Large pinch of sugar
⅓ cup minced fresh chives
Salt and freshly ground black pepper to taste

1½ pounds assorted fresh beans, such as
green beans, yellow wax beans, limas, or favas
½ cup chopped fresh parsley

Soak the dried beans in separate containers in plenty of water to cover overnight, or for quick soaking, bring the beans to a boil in a separate pots with plenty of water, boil 1 minute, cover, and let stand for 1 hour. Drain and cook them separately with water to cover and 1 teaspoon salt in each pot until tender but not mushy, 45 minutes to 1 hour.

Meanwhile, prepare the Chive Vinaigrette. Whisk together the oil, vinegar, mustard, garlic, sugar, chives, and salt and pepper. Set aside until needed.

Steam the fresh beans separately until tender but not limp or mushy, 5 to 7 minutes. Cut long beans into 1-inch pieces. Mix all the cooked beans, dried and fresh, and the parsley together in a large bowl. Pour the vinaigrette over the beans and toss well to combine. Serve at room temperature.

Oven-roasted Asparagus

Kosher and coarse sea salt are a bit too coarse for this dish—grind them down some with a mortar and pestle or the back of a wooden spoon.

3 pounds asparagus
⅓ cup olive oil
Coarse salt

Preheat the oven to 500°. Rinse the asparagus and bend each stalk carefully until it breaks at its natural breaking point (this removes the tough end). Brush the asparagus liberally with olive oil, sprinkle with salt, and arrange in one layer on a baking sheet. Cook the asparagus for 15 minutes, or until crisp-tender. Cool. Serve at room temperature.

VEAL ROAST WITH MARSALA AND DRIED APRICOTS

Grilled Veal Roast with Marsala and Dried Apricots • Pasta with Grilled Mushrooms
Radicchio with Walnut Vinaigrette • Bread Sticks • Red Wine

Serves 6

Tender veal and sweet apricots come together in this beautiful grilled roast with Italian Marsala marinade. The pasta with mushrooms is redolent with garlic and the smoky flavor of the grill.

Grilled Veal Roast with Marsala and Dried Apricots

Opt for the tender meat of a boneless rolled leg roast, if possible. We cook it to an internal temperature of 150° for a tender and juicy roast that is still slightly pink. Leave it on longer for more well-done meat.

> **Marsala and Apricot Marinade, page 42**
> **One 2¾- to 3-pound veal roast,**
>   **preferably a boneless leg roast**
> **8 dried apricots, thinly sliced**
> **1 large shallot, chopped**
> **1 tablespoon fresh thyme leaves,**
>   **or 1 teaspoon dried thyme**

Prepare the Marsala and Apricot Marinade. If the veal roast is tied, untie it. Marinate the roast at room temperature for 2 hours, or longer in the refrigerator.

Combine the apricots, chopped shallot, and thyme. Remove the veal from the marinade, lay it open on a flat surface, and sprinkle the apricot mixture all over it. Roll the veal jelly-roll fashion and tie it with cotton string, tucking in and securing the ends.

On an open grill over red-hot coals, sear the roast for 2 minutes on two sides, and 1 minute each on the other two sides, for a total of 6 minutes. Cover the grill, partially close the vents, and continue cooking the roast for approximately 1 hour. Baste every 10 minutes with the marinade. Turn the roast once halfway through cooking. The roast is done when a thermometer inserted into the thickest part reads 150°, or higher for more well-done meat.

Pasta with Grilled Mushrooms

Use fresh crimini or Italian field mushrooms, or fresh porcini, oyster, or cultivated mushrooms in this recipe.

> **½ cup plus 2 tablespoons virgin olive oil**
> **4 large garlic cloves, cut into large chunks**
> **One ½-inch piece dried red pepper**
> **12 to 18 mushrooms, depending on size**
> **½ tablespoon salt**
> **1½ pounds dried linguine**
> **2 heaping tablespoons chopped fresh Italian parsley**
> **Freshly grated Parmesan cheese**

Heat the olive oil in a small skillet. Add the garlic pieces and dried pepper and cook over very low heat until the garlic begins to turn light brown, approximately 20 minutes. Do not let it burn.

Soak 6 wood skewers in water for 15 minutes.

Meanwhile, bring a large pot of water to a boil and prepare the mushrooms.

Wipe the mushrooms with a damp paper towel and trim the stems. Skewer them horizontally rather than up through the stem and brush with the hot oil. In a covered grill over medium-hot coals, grill the mushrooms for 5 to 7 minutes per side.

While the mushrooms are grilling, add the salt to the boiling water and cook the pasta for 7 minutes, or until al dente. Remove the mushrooms from the grill. Drain the pasta and put it in a large bowl. Unskewer and slice the mushrooms. Remove the red pepper piece and add the hot oil and sliced mushrooms to the pasta, tossing it well to coat. Add the parsley, toss again, and serve with lots of Parmesan cheese.

Radicchio with Walnut Vinaigrette

> **2 heads radicchio**
> **¼ cup walnuts, broken into chunks**
>
> *Walnut Vinaigrette*
>
> **6 tablespoons walnut oil**
> **3 tablespoons champagne vinegar**
> **½ teaspoon Dijon mustard**
> **1 teaspoon orange marmalade**
> **Salt and freshly ground pepper to taste**
> **2 green onions, white part and half the green,**
>   **minced**

Preheat the oven to 375°. Wash and dry the radicchio leaves. Toast the walnuts in the preheated oven for 5 to 7 minutes, or until they are just beginning to darken. Set aside to cool.

Combine the oil, vinegar, mustard, marmalade, and salt and pepper and whisk until emulsified.

Into a large bowl, break the radicchio leaves into pieces and toss with the vinaigrette. Sprinkle each serving with green onions and toasted walnuts.

HICKORY-GRILLED PORK CHOPS WITH FRESH PEACHES

Hickory-grilled Pork Chops with Fresh Peaches • Spicy Black-eyed Peas
Steamed Swiss Chard with Mustard Vinaigrette • Corn Sticks • White Wine

Serves 6

No meat tastes better with fruit than pork, and these savory hickory-flavored chops are delicious with fresh peaches. Here we pay homage to hearty Southern cooking, with black-eyed peas, chard, and crumbly hot corn sticks.

Hickory-grilled Pork Chops with Peaches

If the chops are particularly large, one may be enough to serve 2 people. Nectarines are an excellent substitute if peaches are unavailable.

Beer and Grainy Mustard Marinade, page 42
6 center-cut loin chops, 1¼ inch thick
3 large firm but ripe peaches

Prepare the Beer and Grainy Mustard Marinade.

Marinate the pork chops for 2 hours at room temperature, or longer in the refrigerator.

On an open grill over red-hot coals, sear the chops for 1½ minutes per side. Cover the grill and continue cooking the chops, 8 to 10 minutes on each side.

Peel, pit, and thinly slice the peaches. Serve each chop with several fresh peach slices.

Spicy Black-eyed Peas

If you are short on time and need to quick-soak the peas, place them in a large pot with more than enough water to cover. Bring it to a boil and cook for 2 minutes. Remove the beans from the heat and let stand 1 hour.

2 cups dried black-eyed peas
4 cups water
1 meaty ham hock
1 bay leaf
1 yellow onion, halved and thinly sliced
½ teaspoon cayenne
½ teaspoon salt
1 jalapeño pepper, seeded and minced
Hot sauce to taste

Rinse the peas in a colander and pick out any rocks. Soak them overnight in 3 times as much water.

Drain the peas and put them in a large stockpot. Add the water, ham hock, bay leaf, onion, cayenne, and salt. Bring to a boil, reduce the heat to a simmer, cover, and cook for 45 minutes. Remove the cover and cook the beans another 1 hour and 45 minutes, or until they begin to lose their shape and the sauce is thick.

Toward the end of cooking, remove the ham hock and scrape the meat from the bone. Cut away the fat, chop the hock meat coarsely, and add it to the beans. Stir in the jalapeño and hot sauce to taste.

When the beans are done, adjust the seasoning and serve.

Steamed Swiss Chard with Mustard Vinaigrette

2 bunches Swiss chard

Mustard Vinaigrette
5 tablespoons olive oil
1 tablespoon Dijon-style mustard
2 teaspoons white wine vinegar
Small pinch of sugar
Salt and freshly ground black pepper to taste

Rinse the chard leaves well under running water. Cut out the thick white stem.

Whisk together the remaining ingredients until emulsified.

Steam the chard until tender and wilted, approximately 4 minutes. Toss the cooked chard with the vinaigrette and serve immediately.

Corn Sticks

You will need two cast-iron corn stick pans for this old-fashioned recipe. It will make 12 corn sticks. If you use one pan and cook the corn sticks in two batches, keep the batter chilled until needed.

1¼ cups yellow cornmeal
¾ cup unbleached all-purpose flour
¼ cup brown sugar
2 teaspoons baking powder
½ teaspoon salt
1 cup milk
1 egg, beaten
3 tablespoons butter, melted

Preheat the oven to 425°. Oil the cast-iron corn stick pan and place it in the preheated oven for 3 minutes, or until very hot.

In a medium bowl, combine the dry ingredients and mix well. In another medium bowl, combine the milk, egg, and butter and mix into the dry ingredients, stirring until the batter is smooth.

Remove the hot pan from the oven and spread the batter into the molds, filling them just to the the top. Bake for 12 minutes, or until golden brown.

RABBIT WITH PECAN BUTTER AND APPLES

Grilled Rabbit with Pecan Butter and Apples
Steamed Brussels Sprouts • Gougère • White Wine

Serves 4

The flavor of rabbit has been compared with that of chicken, though the rabbit's all-white meat is leaner, more flavorful, and a bit drier. It is particularly delicious cooked on the grill.

Grilled Rabbit with Pecan Butter and Apples

Look for fresh, young whole rabbits on the smallish side. They should have thin leg bones and white fat. If only frozen rabbit is available, thaw it in the refrigerator overnight.

> **White Wine Marinade, page 39**
> **2 whole rabbits, approximately 3½ pounds each, cleaned**
> **Pecan Butter, page 51**
> **Walnut oil**
> **2 firm red apples**

Prepare the White Wine Marinade.

Place 1 rabbit opened out and flat on a board or counter-top, bone side down. Press firmly with the heel of your hand at the shoulders to flatten. Press again sharply at the haunches (back end) to flatten. Repeat with the other rabbit. Place them in a large flat dish and marinate the rabbits for 4 to 6 hours in the refrigerator.

Prepare the Pecan Butter and set aside.

Bring the rabbits to room temperature and remove from the marinade. Pat dry and brush with oil. Oil the cooking rack. On an uncovered grill over red-hot coals, sear the rabbits skin-side down for 2 minutes. Turn and sear the other side for 2 minutes. Cover the grill, partially close the vents, and continue cooking the rabbits for another 30 minutes, basting occasionally with the marinade. Before the rabbits are done, slice the apples crosswise into ⅓-inch-thick slices, brush with oil, and grill 4 minutes per side.

The rabbits are done when there is no redness to the meat and the internal temperature is 160°. Remove the rabbits and divide each one into 6 pieces (2 legs, 2 shoulders, the rib section, and the loin). Serve over apple slices, with a dollop of Pecan Butter on each piece.

Steamed Brussels Sprouts

> **1 pound small Brussels sprouts**
> **2 tablespoons butter**
> **1 teaspoon dry white wine**

> **2 tablespoons heavy cream or half and half**
> **Several gratings fresh nutmeg**
> **Salt and freshly ground black pepper to taste**

Rinse the Brussels sprouts and pull off any loose or yellowed leaves. Trim and make a ¼-inch-deep X in the base of each with the tip of a sharp knife. Steam for approximately 5 minutes, or until just tender when pierced with a skewer.

Heat the butter and wine in a skillet over medium heat. Add the Brussels sprouts and sauté for 5 minutes. Add the cream, nutmeg, and salt and pepper. Heat and serve immediately.

Gougère

This beautifully puffy, golden-brown wreath is a cheese bread from the Burgundy region of France.

> **1 cup plus 1 tablespoon milk**
> **½ cup (1 stick) unsalted butter, cut into chunks**
> **½ teaspoon salt**
> **1 cup unbleached all-purpose flour**
> **4 eggs**
> **1½ cups grated Gruyère cheese**
> **¼ teaspoon ground nutmeg**
> **Freshly ground black pepper to taste**
> **1 egg yolk**
> **3 tablespoons freshly grated Parmesan cheese**

Preheat the oven to 375°.

In a large saucepan, combine 1 cup of the milk, the butter chunks, and salt. Over medium heat, boil the milk until the butter foams up and immediately remove the pan from the heat. Add the flour all at once and stir vigorously with a wooden spoon. When the mixture forms a doughy ball, return it to medium heat and continue stirring for 2 to 3 minutes. The dough should pull away from the sides of the pan.

Remove the pan from the heat again. Add 1 egg and stir vigorously until it is completely incorporated. Repeat with the other 3 eggs, adding them one at a time.

To the well-mixed dough add the Gruyère, nutmeg, and several grindings of black pepper. Mix well.

Butter a baking sheet. Drop 8 large spoonfuls of dough onto the sheet, forming a ring, with the edges of each ball of dough touching. Beat the egg yolk with the remaining 1 tablespoon of milk and brush this over the surface of the ring. Sprinkle the Parmesan on top.

Bake in the preheated oven for 30 to 35 minutes, or until puffed and golden brown.

MONKFISH WITH CAPER VINAIGRETTE

Grilled Monkfish with Caper Vinaigrette • Grilled Belgian Endive
Steamed Carrots with Cream • French Bread • White Wine

Serves 4

Monkfish is most commonly found in the East Coast's Atlantic waters, and its steady gourmet diet of tender crustaceans has much to do with its sweet, lobsterlike flavor. Low in fat but moist, it has a firm texture that makes it an excellent fish for grilling. In the fish market it may also be called angler or goosefish.

Grilled Monkfish with Caper Vinaigrette

Look for fresh, unfrozen fillets.

> **Caper Vinaigrette, page 48**
> **4 monkfish fillets, ⅓ to ½ pound each (or 1½ pounds monkfish fillet, cut into serving-sized pieces)**
> **Olive oil**

Prepare the Caper Vinaigrette and set aside.

Brush the monkfish liberally with olive oil and oil the cooking rack. On an open grill over red-hot coals, grill the fish for 5 to 7 minutes per side, or until it flakes with a fork and has just lost its translucency in the center. Serve each fillet with a spoonful of vinaigrette on top.

Grilled Belgian Endive

> **4 heads Belgian endive**
> **Olive oil**
> **Salt to taste**

Slice the Belgian endive heads in half lengthwise. Rinse between the leaves, taking care not to separate the leaves from the base. Rub the endive halves generously with olive oil and sprinkle lightly with salt.

On an open grill over medium-hot coals, grill the endive for 3 to 5 minutes per side, or until the base is tender when pierced with a skewer and the leaves are slightly browned and crisp.

Steamed Carrots with Cream

Look for small, fresh, uncracked carrots, or use whole baby carrots.

> **6 to 8 small carrots**
> **3 tablespoons heavy cream**
> **1 teaspoon chopped fresh sage leaves, or ¼ teaspoon dried sage**
> **Salt and freshly ground pepper to taste**

Rinse, trim, and peel the carrots and pat dry. Slice diagonally into ½-inch-thick coins. Steam for 5 minutes, or until just barely tender when pierced with a skewer.

In a small skillet, heat the cream. Add the cooked carrots and cook to reduce the cream for 3 minutes. Add the sage and season with salt and pepper.

STEAK TERIYAKI RICE BOWL

Steak Teriyaki Rice Bowl • Grilled Japanese Eggplant
Spinach-Sesame Salad • Japanese Beer

Serves 4

Our rice bowl is a variation on the Japanese *donburi,* or "big bowl," with grilled teriyaki-marinated steak served over rice with grilled eggplant and green onion.

Steak Teriyaki Rice Bowl

The longer the steak marinates, the less expensive a cut you can use, since the marinade will tenderize and flavor it. Trim most of the fat from the meat.

> **Teriyaki Marinade, page 42**
> **Two ¾-inch-thick steaks, 1 pound each**
> **8 small green onions, white part and half the green**
> **Steamed Rice, following**
> **Grilled Japanese Eggplant, following**

Prepare the Teriyaki Marinade. Place the steaks in a large glass or ceramic dish and pour the marinade over them. Cover with plastic wrap and marinate in the refrigerator all day or overnight. Turn the steaks several times as they marinate.

On an open grill over red-hot to medium-hot coals, cook the steaks 3 to 4 minutes per side for rare, and 4 to 5 minutes per side for medium. Dip the green onions in the marinade and grill them to the side of the grill, slightly away from the intense heat, turning frequently, until lightly colored.

Meanwhile, simmer the remaining marinade gently to slightly reduce. Slice the steaks into thin diagonal strips. Serve the steak slices over the rice with the green onion and grilled eggplant, and drizzle with some of the reduced marinade.

Steamed Rice

Use short- or medium-grain rice for this dish. It can usually be found in the specialty section of your grocery store or in Japanese markets.

> **2 cups unconverted short- or medium-grain rice**
> **3⅓ cups water**
> **½ teaspoon salt**

Put the rice in a strainer and rinse it under running water until the water runs clear. Put the drained rice in a large pot with the water and salt. Over medium-high heat, boil the rice until the surface water has been absorbed and the top of the rice is pitted and bubbly, approximately 6 minutes. Cover the pot with a tight-fitting lid and reduce the heat to as low as possible. Simmer covered for another 10 to 12 minutes. Do not let the rice burn. Remove the pot from the heat and let the rice stand, covered, for about 10 minutes. It should be quite dry.

Grilled Japanese Eggplant

Look for firm, unbruised Japanese eggplants: the long, narrow, purple variety. If unavailable, slice a small globe eggplant into rounds.

> **Teriyaki Marinade, page 42**
> **4 Japanese eggplants, or 1 medium-sized eggplant**

Prepare the Teriyaki Marinade (if you are making the Teriyaki Steak, above, you will have plenty of marinade for the eggplant with one recipe).

Trim the ends of the eggplants if desired and slice in half lengthwise. Dip the eggplant halves into the marinade. On an open grill over red-hot to medium-hot coals, grill the eggplant flesh-side down for 2 to 3 minutes, then turn and grill until browned, approximately 4 minutes more.

Spinach-Sesame Salad

Serve this salad at room temperature.

> **2½ pounds fresh spinach**
> **1 tablespoon white sesame seeds**
> **2 tablespoons rice vinegar or cider vinegar**
> **1 teaspoon soy sauce**
> **½ teaspoon minced fresh ginger**
> **2 drops Asian sesame oil**
> **⅛ teaspoon sugar**

Wash the spinach in several changes of cold water in a sink. Remove the stem from each leaf by pulling up from the base to the tip of the leaf.

Shake off the excess water and put the leaves immediately into a large pot (the water clinging to the leaves will provide enough steaming liquid). Cover and steam the spinach over high heat until the leaves are wilted, approximately 2 minutes, tossing once or twice. Remove from the pot with a slotted spoon and place in a colander. Press the excess moisture out with paper towels. Cool and chop very coarsely.

Toast the sesame seeds in a dry skillet over medium heat until they begin to color. In a small bowl combine the vinegar, soy sauce, ginger, sesame oil, and sugar. Pour this over the spinach and toss well to combine. Drain off the excess liquid and sprinkle toasted sesame seeds on each serving.

THAI BARBECUED CHICKEN

Thai Barbecued Chicken • Snow Peas with Toasted Sesame Dressing
Silver Noodles with Cucumber, Carrot, and Rice Vinegar • Lager

Serves 6

The distinguishing flavor of Thai Barbecued Chicken is garlic, and plenty of it. The tangy taste of the garlic is balanced, however, by other flavors in the marinade: peanuts, coconut milk, palm sugar, cilantro, and *nam pla,* or Thai fish sauce.

Thai Barbecued Chicken

Leave the skin on the chicken, but cut away the excess and trim the fat.

> **Thai Barbecue Marinade, page 42**
> **8 to 12 chicken pieces**

Prepare the Thai Barbecue Marinade.

Toss the chicken pieces in the marinade, coating well. Marinate at room temperature for 2 hours, or longer in the refrigerator.

Oil the cooking rack. In a covered grill over medium-hot coals, grill the chicken bone-side down for 12 minutes. Turn and cook for another 10 to 12 minutes, skin-side down, or until the juices run clear when pricked with a skewer.

Snow Peas with Toasted Sesame Dressing

> ¾ **pound snow peas**
> **1 tablespoon white sesame seeds**
> **1 tablespoon peanut oil**
> **2 drops Asian sesame oil**
> **1 tablespoon soy sauce**
> ½ **teaspoon rice vinegar or cider vinegar**
> **1 small pinch of sugar**
> **1 green onion, white part and half the green, minced**

Rinse the snow peas under running water, and pull off the side strings if the peas seem tough. Steam for 5 minutes, or until tender but still slightly crunchy. Run immediately under cold water to cool, drain on paper towels, and pat dry. Place in a bowl.

Toast the sesame seeds in a dry skillet over medium heat until they begin to color. Combine the peanut oil, sesame oil, soy sauce, vinegar, and sugar in a small bowl. Pour this over the snow peas and toss well to combine. Sprinkle the sesame seeds and green onion on top and toss again.

Silver Noodles with Cucumber, Carrot, and Rice Vinegar

Silver noodles, or bean thread noodles, also called cellophane or glass noodles, are available in the specialty section of some grocery stores, or at Southeast Asian markets. You can break the dry bundles in half before cooking to make the noodles more manageable to eat.

> **1 small cucumber, peeled, seeded, and diced**
> **1 small carrot, peeled and sliced into matchstick-sized pieces**
> ½ **cup rice vinegar or cider vinegar**
> ⅛ **teaspoon chili oil**
> **Small pinch of sugar**
> **6 ounces dried silver noodles**
> **12 red leaf lettuce leaves, rinsed and drained**
> **2 tablespoons chopped fresh cilantro**

In a large bowl, combine the diced cucumber and shredded carrot with the vinegar, chili oil, and sugar.

Bring a large pot of water to a boil. Drop the noodles into the boiling water, turn off the heat, and let stand 10 minutes. Drain in a colander, rinse under cool water, and drain well. Toss the noodles with the vegetables and vinegar. Arrange each serving on a lettuce leaf, and sprinkle with chopped cilantro.

SPIEDINI WITH BALSAMIC MARINADE

Spiedini with Balsamic Marinade • Grilled Fennel • Pasta with Brandy-Basil Cream Sauce
Arugula and Red Leaf Lettuce Salad • Italian Red Wine

Serves 6

Spiedini, or "skewers," are popular in Italy. Different meats and sausages are threaded onto skewers and grilled quickly over hot coals, and served with a wedge of lemon. Our *spiedini* of beef filet and lamb are marinated in Italian balsamic vinegar. Try a Chianti or Barbaresco wine with this menu of grilled meat and pasta.

Spiedini with Balsamic Marinade

Balsamic Marinade, page 41
1½ pounds beef filet, trimmed of fat
    and sliced into 1½-inch cubes
1½ pounds lamb sirloin, trimmed of fat
    and sliced into 1½-inch cubes
1 onion, quartered
2 lemons, sliced into wedges

Prepare the Balsamic Marinade.

Put the cubes of meat into a large glass or ceramic bowl with the marinade and toss well to coat the meat. Marinate for 2 hours at room temperature, or 4 hours in the refrigerator. Remove the meat from the refrigerator 30 minutes before grilling.

Thread the meat onto metal skewers, alternating it occasionally with onion pieces. Grill on an open grill over red-hot coals, turning frequently, for 8 to 10 minutes for rare to medium-rare. Serve with lemon wedges.

Grilled Fennel

The sweetness of fennel is especially delicious when grilled.

3 fennel bulbs
Olive oil

Trim off the feathery fennel leaves, leaving about ½ inch of green on the tops of the fennel bulbs. Slice each bulb in half vertically and rub each half with olive oil. Grill the fennel on an open grill over medium-hot coals for approximately 4 minutes per side. Move to a cooler part of the fire if the fennel begins to get too brown.

Pasta with Brandy-Basil Cream Sauce

1½ cups heavy cream
2 tablespoons brandy or cognac
⅛ teaspoon salt
Freshly ground white pepper to taste
½ tablespoon salt
1½ pounds fresh, dried fresh, or dried tagliatelli
8 large fresh basil leaves, sliced into ribbons
Freshly grated Parmesan cheese

Bring a large pot of water to a boil.

Meanwhile, combine the cream and brandy in a small saucepan. Bring it to a boil, reduce the heat, and simmer gently until reduced by half, approximately 20 minutes. Add ⅛ teaspoon of salt and pepper to taste and keep the sauce warm over very low heat until needed.

Add ½ tablespoon of salt and pasta to the boiling water and cook until the pasta is tender and slightly firm, approximately 7 minutes for dried pasta, 3 to 5 for dried fresh, and only 1 or 2 minutes for fresh.

Drain the pasta and place it immediately in a warm bowl. Add the basil to the sauce and pour it over the pasta. Toss well to combine. Serve with grated Parmesan cheese on the side.

Arugula and Red Leaf Lettuce Salad

Arugula is a peppery-flavored green that adds interest to the simplest salad.

1 bunch arugula
1 head red leaf lettuce

Vinaigrette
6 tablespoons virgin olive oil
1 tablespoon red wine vinegar
Small pinch of sugar
Salt and freshly ground black pepper to taste

Wash and dry the arugula and lettuce and tear into smaller pieces.

In the bottom of a salad bowl, whisk the oil, vinegar, sugar, and salt and pepper together. Place the arugula and lettuce on top and toss just before serving.

SWORDFISH WITH PICO DE GALLO

Grilled Swordfish with Pico de Gallo • Grilled Green Tomatoes
Corn on the Cob • Hard Sourdough Rolls • Beer

Serves 4

Swordfish has an almost beef-like flavor that makes it a natural for the grill. It needs to be cooked quickly over hot coals, so that the inside remains tender and juicy. Its full flavor goes well with spicy Pico de Gallo, a salsa with lime and chilies.

Grilled Swordfish with Pico de Gallo

The further in advance you can prepare the Jalapeño Oil, the more infused and hotter it will be.

Jalapeño Oil, page 45
Pico de Gallo, page 51
4 swordfish steaks, approximately ⅓ pound each

Prepare the Jalapeño Oil and Pico de Gallo and set aside.

Brush the swordfish steaks with Jalapeño Oil and oil the cooking rack. On an open grill over red-hot coals, grill the swordfish steaks for 3 minutes per side, or until the center is just opaque. Take care not to overcook it. Serve with Pico de Gallo on the side.

Grilled Green Tomatoes

Green tomatoes are unripened tomatoes, not the smaller husk-covered tomatillos. Use firm red tomatoes if green ones are unavailable.

3 green tomatoes
Oil
Salt to taste

Rinse the tomatoes and pat dry. Slice crosswise into ½-inch-thick slices. Brush the slices with oil and sprinkle with salt. On an open grill over medium-hot coals, grill the tomatoes for approximately 4 minutes per side, or until lightly grill-marked and tender.

Corn on the Cob

Nothing beats fresh corn for simple eating, but take care not to overcook it.

4 whole ears corn
Butter
Salt and pepper to taste

Bring a large pot of water to a boil.

Remove the husks and silks from each ear of corn and trim the ends, if desired. Drop the corn into the boiling water, cover, and return to a boil. Turn off the heat and let the corn sit in the water, covered, for 5 minutes. Remove, drain, and serve immediately with butter and salt and pepper.

TURKEY BREAST SMOKED WITH CHERRY WOOD

Grilled Turkey Breast Smoked with Cherry Wood • Three-Pepper Relish and Cranberry Chutney
Hearty Vegetable Salad with Herbed Aïoli • Custard Corn Bread • White Wine

Serves 6

Turkey breast cooked indirectly over a wood-scented fire, with aromatics like orange peel, peppercorns, garlic, and herbs to flavor the steam, makes a moist and juicy roast. The wood chip smoke mingles with the steam from the liquid, infusing the turkey with flavor and moistness. Experiment with wood chip flavoring by using hickory, apple, or other chips to find what you like best.

Grilled Turkey Breast Smoked with Cherry Wood

If possible, select a whole fresh turkey breast with the bone in. Allow a frozen turkey breast to thaw slowly in the refrigerator for a day. You will need 2 cups of cherry wood chips.

One 5-pound turkey breast
4 bacon slices
1¼ cups dry white wine
2¼ cups water
3 bay leaves
Several large pieces orange peel
8 peppercorns
4 garlic cloves, slightly crushed
Several fresh herb sprigs, such as sage, marjoram, thyme, rosemary, or oregano

Rinse the turkey breast under running water. Pat dry. Drape the bacon slices horizontally across the turkey breast.

Place 2 cups of cherry wood chips in water to cover for 30 minutes. Light the grill. When the charcoal is lit, move it to the sides of the fuel grate or firebox, leaving a space large enough to accommodate a water pan.

Combine the water and wine in a pitcher. Place a water pan on the fuel grate and pour the liquid into the pan, taking care not to splash the hot coals. Add the bay leaves, orange peel, peppercorns, garlic, and herbs to the liquid. Cover the grill and allow the coals to burn down to medium-hot and the liquid to heat up.

Scatter a handful of dampened wood chips on the coals. With the cover on the grill and the vents partially closed, cook the turkey breast skin-side up without turning for 3 to 4 hours, or until a thermometer inserted into the thickest portion reads 165°. Remove the bacon strips halfway through cooking to allow the turkey to brown. While the turkey is cooking, scatter soaked wood chips on the fire from time to time, and replenish the fire with hot coals when necessary.

Remove the turkey from the grill, and cover with a foil tent for 5 minutes before carving.

Hearty Vegetable Salad with Herbed Aïoli

If any of these vegetables look less than desirable in the market, try substituting potatoes, broccoli, artichoke hearts, Belgian endive, or whatever looks appealing.

Herbed Aïoli, page 53
½ cauliflower, separated into florets
2 carrots, peeled and sliced into irregular pieces
¾ pound green beans, cut into 1-inch pieces
6 baby turnips, halved, or 1 large turnip, sliced into ¾-inch-thick chunks
6 small pattypan squash, sliced into ¾-inch-thick chunks
Salt and freshly ground black pepper to taste

Prepare the Herbed Aïoli and set aside.

Steam all the vegetables separately until just tender but not limp or mushy. Cool quickly under cold water and pat dry. Combine the vegetables in a large bowl and pour the aïoli over them. Toss gently to coat the vegetables. Season with salt and pepper.

Custard Corn Bread

1 cup yellow cornmeal
½ cup unbleached all-purpose flour
2 tablespoons dark brown sugar
1 teaspoon baking soda
½ teaspoon salt
2 eggs
1 cup buttermilk
1½ cups milk
1 cup fresh, defrosted frozen, or canned corn kernels
2 tablespoons butter

Preheat the oven to 400°.

In a large bowl, combine the cornmeal, flour, brown sugar, baking soda, and salt and mix well. In another bowl, beat the eggs, buttermilk, and 1 cup of the milk. Add this to the cornmeal mixture and mix gently until just moistened. Stir in the corn kernels. Do not overmix. The batter will be somewhat lumpy.

In a 10-inch cast-iron skillet, melt the butter over low heat and swirl to coat the sides of the pan. Pour the batter into the skillet and drizzle the remaining ½ cup milk over the top.

Bake the cornbread in the skillet for 35 minutes, or until the top is browned. Cut into wedges and serve immediately. The cornbread will have a custardy center.

SEA BASS ON BOK CHOY WITH GINGER-GARLIC BUTTER

Grilled Sea Bass on Bok Choy with Ginger-Garlic Butter • Peanut-Sesame Noodles
Steamed Chinese Long Beans • White Wine

Serves 4

Sea bass is particularly delicious grilled—the high heat of the coals seals in the juices and keeps it moist and tender. Try any fresh, firm white fish in this recipe, such as red snapper, rockfish, cod, or monkfish.

Grilled Sea Bass on Bok Choy with Ginger-Garlic Butter

If baby bok choy is unavailable, use the tender inner leaves of mature bok choy or green leaf lettuce.

> **Ginger-Garlic Butter, page 50**
> **2 heads baby bok choy**
> **2 to 4 sea bass steaks, depending on size**

Prepare the Ginger-Garlic Butter.

Rinse the bok choy leaves and trim the stems. Pat dry and set aside.

Melt 4 tablespoons of the butter in a small saucepan. Brush the sea bass steaks with the butter and set aside for 15 minutes.

Grill the sea bass on an open grill over red-hot coals for 6 to 8 minutes per side, or until the fish just begins to flake and the center is just opaque. Cover the grill if the steaks are particularly thick. Baste the fish several times while it cooks.

Arrange the fish on several bok choy leaves and put a dollop of Ginger-Garlic Butter on each serving.

Peanut-Sesame Noodles

Serve these noodles warm or at room temperature.

> **¼ cup sesame seeds**
> **¾ cup chicken broth**
> **⅓ cup smooth natural unsalted peanut butter**
> **3 tablespoons rice vinegar or cider vinegar**
> **1 tablespoon tamari or soy sauce**
> **2 teaspoons Asian sesame oil**
> **2 tablespoons peanut oil**
> **1 teaspoon chili oil, or to taste**
> **¾ pound thin Chinese egg noodles,**
> **   preferably fresh**
> **1 small cucumber, peeled, seeded, and diced**
> **4 green onions, white part and half the green,**
> **   minced**
> **½ cup roasted salted peanuts, chopped**

Toast the sesame seeds in a dry skillet over medium heat until they begin to color.

In a small saucepan, whisk the sesame seeds, chicken broth, peanut butter, vinegar, tamari, and oils together until well blended. Heat gently but do not boil.

Bring a large pot of water to a boil. Boil the egg noodles according to the package instructions, or until tender. Drain the noodles and toss immediately with the warm sauce.

Sprinkle each serving with cucumber, green onion, and chopped peanuts.

Steamed Chinese Long Beans

Chinese long beans can be found in Asian markets or in the produce section of some supermarkets. They are often over a foot long, and, though they are somewhat droopy even when fresh, they should not be withered or blemished. Green beans may be substituted.

> **1 tablespoon peanut oil**
> **2 drops Asian sesame oil**
> **1 tablespoon tamari or soy sauce**
> **1 teaspoon rice vinegar or cider vinegar**
> **½ garlic clove, minced to a paste**
> **Pinch of sugar**
> **½ pound Chinese long beans or green beans,**
> **   cut into 6-inch pieces**

In a small bowl, whisk together the oils, tamari or soy sauce, vinegar, garlic, and sugar.

Rinse and trim the beans. Steam for 3 to 5 minutes, or until tender but slightly crunchy. Put in a bowl and pour the oil mixture over the hot beans. Toss well. Cool to room temperature and serve.

HICKORY-SMOKED COUNTRY-STYLE RIBS WITH BARBECUE SAUCE

Hickory-smoked Country-style Ribs with Barbecue Sauce
Herbed Twice-baked Potatoes • Wilted Red Cabbage Salad • Beer

Serves 12

This menu is designed for a large, hungry group, great for a special summer occasion. The recipe for ribs was created by Jeff and Debi McMains for Hasty-Bake, their line of gourmet outdoor charcoal grills.

Hickory-smoked Country-style Ribs with Barbecue Sauce

1½ recipes of Spicy Barbecue Shake, page 46
A double recipe of Bourbon Barbecue Sauce, page 48
14 pounds country-style pork ribs
2 onions, minced
8 garlic cloves, minced
½ cup soy sauce
½ cup Worcestershire sauce
Plenty of freshly ground black pepper

Prepare the Spicy Barbecue Shake and the Bourbon Barbecue Sauce.

Rub the shake on all sides of the ribs and place them in a large bowl. Distribute the minced onion and garlic evenly over the ribs. Combine the soy and Worcestershire sauces and drizzle the mixture over the ribs, tossing well. Sprinkle with pepper. Marinate for 2 hours at room temperature, or longer in the refrigerator.

Thirty minutes before cooking, soak 6 hickory wood chunks in water. In a covered grill over a low fire, cook the ribs bone-side down for 3 hours, or until tender and juicy and deeply colored. Add dampened hickory wood chunks to the fire while cooking, and add more charcoal as needed. Baste the ribs with the barbecue sauce toward the end of cooking. Serve the cooked ribs with barbecue sauce on the side.

Herbed Twice-baked Potatoes

14 russet potatoes
Olive oil
½ cup (1 stick) butter, cut into cubes
¾ cup sour cream
¾ cup half and half
8 green onions, white part and half the green, minced
2 garlic cloves, minced to a paste with a pinch of salt
1 tablespoon fresh thyme leaves,
 or 2 teaspoons dried thyme
1 tablespoon chopped fresh sage leaves,
 or 2 teaspoons dried sage
⅓ cup chopped fresh parsley
Salt and freshly ground black pepper to taste
½ cup freshly grated Parmesan cheese

Preheat the oven to 400°.

Scrub the potatoes but do not peel. Rub them with olive oil and prick each potato deeply in several places with a skewer. Bake for 1½ hours in the preheated oven. Place the cubed butter in a large bowl.

Remove the potatoes from the oven. Holding each potato with a hotpad, make a lengthwise slit in the top and scoop the cooked potato into the bowl with the butter. Avoid tearing the potato skins. Set the empty potato shells aside until needed.

Mash the potato with the butter. Add the sour cream and half and half and mash well until mostly smooth. Add the green onions, garlic, thyme, sage, and parsley and mix well. Season to taste with salt and pepper.

Generously refill 12 of the potato shells with the mashed potato. Sprinkle the grated Parmesan on top. Reheat in a 350° oven for 20 minutes, 15 to 20 minutes longer if the potatoes have been prepared ahead and chilled.

Wilted Red Cabbage Salad

1½ heads red cabbage
½ cup olive oil
2 red onions, halved and thinly sliced
4 garlic cloves, minced to a paste
1 tablespoon herbes de Provence or dried thyme
1 teaspoon fennel seed
⅓ cup cider vinegar
1 heaping tablespoon sugar
½ pound feta cheese
½ cup chopped fresh parsley
Salt and freshly ground black pepper to taste

Remove any wilted outer leaves from the cabbage heads. Quarter the heads and cut out the white core. Slice the quarters into thin strips.

Heat the oil in a large pot over medium-high heat. Add the onions and sauté until tender, about 3 minutes. Add the garlic and sauté another minute. Add the herbes de Provence, fennel seed, and cabbage and toss well to coat the strips with hot oil. Sprinkle the vinegar and sugar over the cabbage and continue cooking it, tossing it in the pot until the cabbage is wilted, about 6 minutes. Remove the cabbage to a large bowl.

Crumble the feta cheese into the cabbage, add the parsley, and toss well to combine. Season to taste with salt and pepper. Serve warm or at room temperature.

EQUIPMENT SOURCES

Grill Manufacturers

Check with any of these grill manufacturers for mail-order information or for a distributor near you.

Arkla
P.O. Box 1467
Paragould, AR 72451
(800) 356-3612
All sizes of outdoor gas grills.

Barbecue Time, Inc.
P.O. Box 13637
Portland, OR 97213
(503) 249-6996
Double portable tabletop grills.

Brinkmann Smoke'N Grill
Brinkmann Corp.
4215 McEwen Road
Dallas, TX 75244
(800) 527-0717
Electric smoker and grill.

Broilmaster
Locke Home Products, Inc.
P.O. Box 1040
Washington Park, IL 62204
(618) 271-1272
All sizes of outdoor gas grills.

Char-Broil
W.C. Bradley Enterprises
P.O. Box 1300
Columbus, GA 31993
(800) 241-8981
All sizes of charcoal and gas grills, smokers, and a wide range of accessories.

Charglo
Thermador/Waste King
5119 District Boulevard
Los Angeles, CA 90040
(213) 560-6444
(800) 767-4356
Indoor gas grills.

Charmglow
500 S. Madison
Duquoin, IL 62832
(618) 542-4781
All sizes of outdoor gas grills, smokers, and gas grill accessories.

Cook'n Cajun
P.O. Box 3726
Shreveport, LA 71133
(318) 925-6933
Charcoal-water, electric, and gas smokers.

Ducane
800 Dutch Square Boulevard
Columbia, SC 29210-7376
(803) 798-1600
All sizes of outdoor gas grills.

The Grillery
Grillworks, Inc.
1211 Ferdon Road
Ann Arbor, MI 48104
(313) 995-2164
Gourmet wood cooker for outdoors and fireplace.

Hasty-Bake
4733 S. Memorial
Tulsa, OK 74145
(800) 4AN-OVEN
Fine gourmet charcoal ovens of all sizes. Built-ins for indoors and outdoors also available.

J & R Manufacturing
P.O. Box 850522
Mesquite, TX 75185-0522
(800) 527-4831
Woodburning smoking pits.

Jenn-Air
3035 N. Shadeland
Indianapolis, IN 46226
(317) 545-2271
Indoor gas and electric grills.

Kamado
BSW, Inc.
4680 East Second Street
Benicia, CA 94510
(707) 745-8175
Traditional Japanese earthenware oven/barbecue/smoker.

Little Chief
Luhr-Jensen & Sons
P.O. Box 297
Hood River, OR 97031
(503) 386-3811
Electric smokers.

Meco
P.O. Box 1000
1500 Industrial Road
Greenville, TN 37744-1000
(800) 251-7558
Charcoal and electric grills and smokers.

Pyramid Outdoor Cooking Systems
Lazer Blazer Barbecue
3292 S. Highway 97
Redmond, OR 97756
(800) 824-4288

Sears/Kenmore
See your local directory for the nearest store. Outdoor charcoal and gas grills.

Smokey Bayou Outdoor Cooker
Henkel, Inc.
P.O. Box 1322
Hammond, LA 70404
(504) 345-1016
Large charcoal oven/grill.

Structo
The Thermos Company
Freeport, IL 61032
(815) 232-2111
Portables, braziers, and charcoal and electric grills.

Sunbeam
Sunbeam Leisure Products, Co.
4101 Howard Bush Drive
Neosho, MO 64850
(800) 641-4500
All sizes of outdoor gas grills and gas grill accessories.

Tuscan Grill
Cafe Fanny Imports
1619 5th Street
Berkeley, CA 94610
(415) 526-7664
Adjustable wrought-iron fireplace grill.

Weber
Weber-Stephens Products Company
200 East Daniels Road
Palatine, IL 60067
(800) 323-7598
All sizes of charcoal and gas kettle grills and accessories.

Fuel Sources

These charcoal and wood chip and chunk distributors will sell by mail-order or will direct you to their nearest retailers.

Connecticut Charcoal Company
Old Time Charcoal
(203) 684-3208
Pure hardwood charcoal.

Desert Mesquite of Arizona
3458 E. Illini Street
Phoenix, AZ 85040
(602) 437-3135
Mesquite chips and chunks, sawdust.

Humphrey Charcoal Corporation
P.O. Box 440
Brookville, PA 15825
(814) 849-2302
Pure hardwood charcoal and hardwood
charcoal briquets.

Lazzari Fuel Company
P.O. Box 34051
San Francisco, CA 94034
(415) 467-2970 (within California)
(800) 242-7265 (outside of California)
Pure mesquite charcoal from Mexico.
Apple, cherry, alder, olive, hickory, and
mesquite chips; hickory and mesquite
wood chunks.

Luhr Jensen & Sons, Inc.
P.O. Box 297
Hood River, OR 97031
(503) 386-3811
Hickory, alder, cherry, and apple chips.

Tool Sources
*Call these tool manufacturers and distributors
for a retailer in your area.*

Char-chef
Char Star
P.O. Box 690026
Tulsa, OK 74169
(918) 663-0700
Chimneys.

Charcoal Companion
1150 Sixth Street
Oakland, CA 94710
(415) 525-3800
Chimneys, grill thermometers, tongs,
forks, brushes, and more.

Griffo-grill Inc.
301 Oak Street
Quincy, IL 62301
(800) 426-1286
All sizes of high-quality stainless steel
grill racks and hinged grill baskets.

Outdoor Chef
P.O. Box 6255
Evansville, IN 47719-0255
(800) 544-5362
All types of tools, equipment, and parts
for charcoal and gas grills.

Weber
Weber-Stephens Product Company
200 East Daniels Road
Palatine, IL 60067
(800) 323-7598
Equipment for Weber grills and all types
of grilling tools.

BIBLIOGRAPHY

California Culinary Academy. *Barbecuing, Grilling & Smoking.* San Ramon, CA: Ortho Information Services, Chevron Chemical Company, 1988.

Campbell, Susan. *Cook's Tools.* New York: Bantam Books, 1980.

The Editors of Sunset Books. *Barbecue Cookbook.* Menlo Park, CA: Lane Publishing Company, 1983.

The Editors of Time-Life Books. *Outdoor Cooking.* Alexandria, VA: Time-Life Books, 1983.

Ellis, Merle. *Cutting-up in the Kitchen.* San Francisco, CA: Chronicle Books, 1975.

Hodgson, Moira. *The New York Times Gourmet Shopper.* New York: Times Books, 1983.

Tannahill, Reay. *Food in History.* New York: Stein and Day, 1973.

GRILL BOOK
List of Menus

Butterflied Leg of Lamb with Zinfandel Sauce
Grilled Turnips
Braised Spinach with Toasted Almonds
Crusty Italian Bread

Veal Chops with Gruyère and Prosciutto
Grilled Polenta with Pesto
Grilled Pattypan Squash
Roasted Red Pepper Salad

Skewered Scallops, Zucchini, and Artichoke Hearts with Salsa
Herbed Rice
Cold Lemon Asparagus

Grilled Whole Trout
Grilled Mixed Vegetables with Aïoli
Arugula, Limestone, and Red Leaf Lettuce Salad with Avocado

Grilled Steak with Fresh Herbs
Grilled Sweet Corn
Caesar Salad
Sourdough Bread

Salmon Steaks with Chive Butter
Grilled Japanese Eggplant
Grilled Scallions
Cold Pasta Salad

Tofu Marinated in Sesame Oil and Rice Vinegar with Scallions
Grilled Whole Chilies
Sliced Fresh Fruit
Cold Soba Noodles

Rock Cornish Game Hens in Raspberry Vinegar Marinade
Grilled Pears
Grilled Mushrooms
Steamed Fresh Green Beans with Water Chestnuts

Sesame Flank Steak
Grilled Whole Potatoes
Sautéed Fresh Okra
Sliced Tomatoes with Olive Oil and Basil

Boneless Pork Loin in Sherry Vinegar, Port, and Prune Marinade
Grilled Carrots
Herbed Potatoes
Tossed Greens

Grilled Split Lobster Tail
Roasted Garlic Heads
Butter Lettuce and Watercress Salad
Baguette

Mixed Sausage Grill
Grilled Red Onion Quarters
Red Cabbage with Apples
Dark German Bread

Chicken Breasts in Many Mustards
Grilled Gravenstein Apple Slices
Grilled Baby Leeks
Radicchio Salad

Nam Prik Shrimp
Grilled Zucchini
Tomato Pasta with Olive Oil and Lemon Zest

Grilled Breast of Duck in Red Wine Marinade
Grilled Crookneck Squash
Wild Rice with Green Onions and Mushrooms
Belgian Endive Salad with Toasted Pine Nuts

Peanut Chicken on Skewers
Rice with Lemon Grass and Coconut
Carrot Salad with Green Papaya

Barbecued Baby Back Pork Ribs in Honey, Tamari, and Orange Marinade
Grilled Yam Slices
Waldorf Salad
Corn Muffins with Green Chilies

Grill Appetizer Party
Topinka
Grilled Oysters and Clams on the Shell

INDEX

*This book was
composed in Bembo types by
On Line Typography,
San Francisco*

*It was printed
and bound by
Dai Nippon Printing Co. Ltd.
Tokyo, Japan*

*Design & production by
Thomas Ingalls + Associates
San Francisco*